THE

CHILDREN ON THE TOP FLOOR

BY

NINA RHOADES

Contents

CHAPTER I

A MISHAP AND ITS CONSEQUENCES

"Will you please let me have two cream cakes?"

The young woman behind the counter of the small bakery glanced kindly at the maker of this request, a little girl in a rather neat-looking dress, with a dark, earnest face and a pair of big, solemn brown eyes.

"They're nice and fresh to-day," she remarked pleasantly; "they came out of the oven only an hour ago."

The customer smiled.

"I'm glad," she said; "my little brother is very fond of cream cakes."

"And how is your little brother to-day?" the woman questioned, at the same time selecting three large, fat cream cakes from the heaped up dish on the counter.

"He's pretty well, thank you. Oh, excuse me, but you're giving me three; I only asked for two."

"Never mind about that, it's all right. Too bad your little brother can't get out these fine spring days, isn't it?"

A troubled, wistful look came into the child's face.

"He would like to get out," she said sadly; "I wish he could."

"Yes, indeed, I don't wonder; it's just grand in the park these warm afternoons. My two little boys about live there. If you could take him out for a drive sometimes, it would do him a lot of good, I'm sure."

Before the child could answer, the door of the bakery opened, and two more customers, a lady and a little girl of nine or ten, came in.

"Well, Winnie," said the lady smiling, as they approached the counter, "have you decided which it is to be to-day, macaroons or chocolate éclairs?"

"I think it had better be éclairs to-day, we had macaroons three times last week," the little girl said, laughing, and glancing with an expression of interest at the first customer, who had now received her package, and was turning to leave the store. "Oh, mother," she added eagerly, as the door closed, "did you see? that's the little girl who lives in our house."

"Was it really?" the lady inquired, looking interested in her turn; "I didn't notice her."

"Oh, yes, I'm quite sure; I've seen her several times on the stairs, you know. I wish she hadn't gone so quick; I should have liked to speak to her. It seems so queer not to know a person who lives in the same house that you do, doesn't it?"

"And a very nice little girl she is too," put in the young woman behind the counter, glad of an opportunity to say a good word for one of her favorite customers. "She often comes in here, and we serve the family with bread. They live in the apartment house on the corner."

"That's where we live," said Winifred; "do you know what the little girl's name is?"

"Yes; it's Randall, Betty Randall; she told me so herself the other day. Her mother's a very handsome lady, quite stylish-looking, though I believe she gives lessons of some kind. She's a widow, with two children, this one and a little boy, who is a cripple. It's my opinion they've seen better days. Shall I send these things, ma'am, or will you take them with you?"

"I will take them, thank you. Come, Winifred."

"Mother," said Winifred, as they left the bakery, "I really do wish I knew that little girl. She has a very nice face, and if her brother is a cripple, I might go and read to him sometimes. You know I'm very fond of cripples."

The lady laughed.

"Well, you may speak to the child, if you like," she said kindly. "I scarcely know whether it would do for you to call on the family. You see, dear, a great many people live in that big apartment house, and they may not all be desirable friends for you. But look, isn't that the very child you are talking about? Yes, to be sure it is, and she seems to be in trouble. She must have had a fall."

A moment later little Betty Randall, standing in the middle of the sidewalk, gazing disconsolately down on the débris of her three cream cakes, which lay crushed and shapeless at her feet, was startled to hear a sweet, sympathetic voice saying close to her side:

"I'm sorry; how did it happen?"

"I slipped on a piece of orange peel," explained little Betty, at once recognizing the lady and little girl she had seen at the baker's, "and fell right on my bag of cream cakes. They're all spoiled."

Little Betty Randall gazing disconsolately down on the débris of her three cream cakes.

"It's too bad, but hadn't you better go back for some more?" the lady suggested pleasantly.

Betty hesitated, and her color rose.

"I think not to-day," she said a little primly; "mother might not like it. I don't mind about myself," she added quickly, "but I'm sorry for Jack; he's very fond of cream cakes."

"Is Jack your little brother?" Winifred asked.

"Yes; how did you know I had a little brother?"

"The woman at the baker's said so, and she said he was a cripple."

Betty's face softened wonderfully. By this time they had abandoned the cream cakes to their fate, and were all three walking on together towards the big apartment house on the next corner.

"Yes, he is a cripple," she said; "he can't walk at all. He had a fall when he was a baby, and it hurt his spine."

"How very sad," said Winifred sympathetically; "how did it happen?"

"His nurse dropped him one day when mother and father were out. She didn't tell at first, and nobody knew what was the matter with Jack, and what made him cry whenever any one touched him. At last the doctor found out that his spine was injured, and then she confessed."

"How old is he now?" Winifred inquired.

"He will be nine the day after to-morrow, but he seems older than that. He's a very clever little boy; he reads a great deal, and he can draw beautiful pictures. Mother thinks it's because he is so much by himself that he gets to be so old-fashioned. I'm eleven, but I'm not nearly so clever as Jack."

"I suppose you are very fond of him," said Winifred. "A person would naturally be very fond of a brother who is a cripple."

"I love him better than anything else in the world," said Betty simply.

At that moment the apartment house was reached.

"Isn't it strange that we live in the same house and never spoke to each other before?" remarked Winifred, as they mounted the first flight of stairs together. "We haven't lived here very long, though; only since January."

"We have lived here for two years," said Betty, "and we don't know any of the people in the house."

Winifred's eyes opened wide in surprise, but they were already on the first landing, and her mother had rung the bell of their own apartment.

"Good-bye," she said, "this is where we live. I hope I shall see you again soon."

Betty stood for a moment gazing at the closed door, behind which her new acquaintances had disappeared, and then she toiled on, up three more long steep flights of stairs, until, on the very top landing of all, she paused, and taking a key from her pocket, proceeded to open a door on her right.

"Is that you, Betty?" called an eager little voice, as the door swung open, and Betty passed into the small, narrow hall of the "top floor rear apartment."

"Yes, dear; but, oh, Jack, I'm so sorry; I slipped on a horrid piece of orange peel and spilled all the cream cakes. It'll have to be cold meat and bread and butter to-day."

"You didn't hurt yourself, did you?" the anxious little voice inquired.

"Oh, no, not a bit, and quite an interesting thing happened. Just wait till I take off my hat, and get your lunch ready, and I'll tell you all about it."

Five minutes later, Betty, her little dark face somewhat flushed from recent exertions, but looking, on the whole, very bright and happy, entered the small front room, bearing a tray containing milk, cold meat, and a pile of thin bread-and-butter sandwiches.

"I'll put it on the little table, and we can have lunch together," she said cheerfully. "See what a lot of sandwiches mother's made for us."

As she spoke, Betty drew a small table close to the sofa on which lay the little cripple. Jack watched her every movement with loving eyes. Such a pale, wan face as it was; such a poor, shrunken little body! But it was not a dull face, and the large, beautiful blue eyes had a bright, glad light in them, despite the fact that their owner spent all his poor life confined to a sofa.

"Now tell me about the interesting thing," Jack said, when Betty, having completed her arrangements, had seated herself by his side, prepared to enjoy the cold meat and bread and butter.

"Yes, I will. It isn't very much, though, only when I was at the baker's who should happen to come in but the lady and the little girl who live down on the second floor. You know, I told you about that little girl, how pretty she was, and how she and her mother were always together. I've seen her mother taking her to school ever so many mornings, and I think she was on her way home from school now, for she carried books. Well, I got my cream cakes—they were lovely ones too, and the woman gave me three, though I only asked for two—and I was hurrying home as fast as I could, when all of a sudden I slipped on that old orange peel, and fell flat. My bag burst open, and of course the cream cakes were all squashed. I got up, and was standing looking at my poor cream cakes, and feeling so dreadfully sorry, when the lady and the little girl stopped to speak to me. They were ever so kind. The lady said I had better go back to the store for more, but I didn't have money enough for that, you know."

"You didn't say so, did you?" Jack questioned anxiously.

"Of course I didn't. I just said I thought I wouldn't go back to-day, and then we all walked home together, and the little girl asked me about you."

"What did you tell her?"

"Oh, I said you were a very clever boy, and—why, there's the door bell; I wonder who it can be?"

"Perhaps it's mother come home early," Jack suggested, his pale little face brightening; "perhaps one of her pupils didn't take a lesson, or——"

But Betty did not hear. She was already halfway across the little hall, and in another moment was standing with the open door in her hand, gazing in surprise at the neat, pleasant-faced servant girl who confronted her. The girl held in her hand a plate covered with a napkin.

"Is this Miss Betty Randall?" the stranger inquired, smiling.

"Yes," said Betty, in growing bewilderment. She was sure she had never seen the girl before.

"Well, here are some éclairs for you. Miss Winifred Hamilton sends them to you and your little brother, and hopes you'll both enjoy them."

And before Betty could recover sufficiently from her surprise to utter a word of either thanks or protest, the plate was in her hands, and the servant girl was hurrying away downstairs.

It was with a very bright face, however, that the little girl came running back into the sitting room, in answer to Jack's eager "What is it, Betty?"

"It's éclairs, four beautiful chocolate éclairs," she explained joyfully, "and the nice little girl downstairs has sent them to us.

"She just bought them too, for I heard her mother asking her at the baker's whether it was to be éclairs or macaroons, and she said éclairs. Wasn't it kind of her to send them? You do like chocolate éclairs very much, don't you, Jack, dear?"

"I love them," said Jack heartily, "but, Betty, do you suppose mother would like it?"

Betty's bright face clouded, but only for a moment.

"I don't believe she'd mind," she said with decision. "You see, things to eat aren't like money, and I think it would be rude not to take them when the little girl was so kind."

Jack acquiesced in this view of the matter, and the two children were soon in the full enjoyment of their unexpected treat.

"Her name is Hamilton, Winifred Hamilton," remarked Betty, poising a delicious morsel on her fork as she spoke, "and she knows my name too. The maid asked if I wasn't Miss Betty Randall. She is such a pretty little girl, Jack; her hair is all fluffy and crimpy round her face, and she's got beautiful eyes."

"I wish I could see her," said Jack wistfully; "do you suppose she would come up here if you asked her?"

"I shouldn't wonder," said Betty hopefully; "she said she was very much interested in cripples."

Jack made an impatient movement, and a look of pain crossed his face.

"I wish I wasn't a cripple," he said, his lip beginning to tremble; "I wish I could get up and walk like other people. I want to see things."

Betty laid down her fork, and a look of sympathy and almost womanly tenderness came into her eyes.

"What kind of things do you want to see, Jack?" she asked gently.

"Oh, I don't know; all kinds of things. I get so tired looking out of the window at roofs and chimneys. I should like to see a park with deer in it, and swans and a peacock, like the one mother tells about."

"But you couldn't see that park, you know, dear, because that was in England, away across the Atlantic Ocean."

"Well, but there is a park here, too, isn't there? I heard Mrs. Flynn talking about it the other day. She said it was beautiful in the park now, with all the flowers coming out."

"Oh, yes, there's Central Park, and it is very pretty, but not so pretty as the one mother tells about."

Jack's face brightened again.

"Couldn't I go there some time?" he asked eagerly; "is it too far for any one to carry me?"

Betty shook her head sadly.

"I'm afraid it's too far for that," she admitted, "but if we only had a carriage you could go. The janitor would carry you downstairs, I know, and it wouldn't be a long drive. I don't believe it would hurt your back one bit. I'll tell you what, Jack. Day after to-morrow will be your birthday; let's ask mother to hire a carriage, and take us both."

Betty's eyes were sparkling with the sudden inspiration, but now it was Jack's turn to shake his head and look dubious.

"I'm afraid it would cost too much," he said mournfully; "I should love it, but I'm really afraid it would."

"I don't believe it would be so very expensive," said hopeful Betty. "There's a livery stable right across the street, and I'll go over this afternoon and find out how much it costs. I've got a dollar and five cents in my bank; I counted it last night, and mother says it's all mine, to do just what I please with. Oh, Jack, dear, I'm sure it can't cost more than a dollar, and I should just love to get it for your birthday present. I wonder why we were all so stupid as never to have thought of doing it before."

CHAPTER II

BETTY'S TEMPTATION

It was about an hour later when Betty, having washed and put away the luncheon dishes, and settled Jack with his story book and drawing materials, ran lightly down the three long flights of stairs to the Hamiltons' apartment. In one hand she carried Mrs. Hamilton's plate and napkin, and in the other a small tin money box, which jingled at every step. At the Hamiltons' front door she paused, and rather timidly rang the bell. The door was opened by the same girl who had brought the éclairs.

"I came to bring back the plate," Betty explained, "and will you please tell Miss Winifred Hamilton that my little brother and I enjoyed the cakes very much."

"Wouldn't you like to come in and speak to her yourself?" the girl asked pleasantly; "she's right here."

She moved aside as she spoke, and there, sure enough, was Winifred standing smiling in the parlor door.

"Yes, do come in," said the little girl hospitably. "Mother's out, but I stayed at home to make a dress for one of my children. They're really my *dolls*, you know," she added, smiling at Betty's look of bewilderment, "but I always call them my children. I'm so very fond of them, you see, and they do seem something like real children. Come in and I'll show them to you."

There was no declining this tempting invitation, and Betty was soon making the acquaintance of Winifred's family, and being introduced respectively to Lord Fauntleroy, Rose-Florence, Violet-May, Lily-Bell, and Miss Mollie.

"You see, when my father and mother were away in California I used to be alone a good deal," Winifred explained, "and so if it hadn't been for the children I should have been rather lonely. I lived with Uncle Will and Aunt Estelle then, and Aunt Estelle is a very busy lady and has to go out a good deal. My mother hardly ever goes out without me, and I don't have nearly so much time to devote to the children as I used, but I shouldn't like to have them feel neglected, so sometimes I stay at home on purpose to look after them a little."

"How old are you?" Betty inquired. To her this conversation seemed extremely childish. She had never had much time in her busy little life to care for dolls, Jack having claimed all her thought and attention.

"I shall be ten next July, so as it's April now, father says I'm nine and three-quarters. Father's very fond of joking, and so is Uncle Will."

"You go to school, don't you?" Betty asked.

"Yes, I go to Miss Lothrop's. I was coming from school when I met you to-day. Mother almost always takes me and comes for me herself, because we have only Lizzie, and she has a great deal to do."

"We don't keep any girl at all now," said Betty, "and so I can't go to school, because there would be nobody to take care of Jack. We did keep a girl last year, but some of mother's pupils gave up, and she couldn't get any new ones, so we had to let her go. Mother gives us our lessons every afternoon when she comes home, and we study in the mornings by ourselves."

"Is your mother a teacher?" Winifred inquired with interest.

"Yes, she gives music lessons, and she plays beautifully too. We have a piano, because Jack loves music so, and mother plays to him almost every evening."

"I guess cripples always like music," said Winifred reflectively. "Mr. Bradford had a lovely music box; it played twelve tunes."

"Who is Mr. Bradford?"

"He was a crippled gentleman I used to know. He was very kind, and I loved him very much. I used to read to him, and he liked it. He died last winter."

"Some cripples are quite strong in other ways, you know," Betty hastened to explain. Winifred's remark about dying had made her vaguely uncomfortable. "Jack isn't nearly so delicate as he used to be. I think if he could only get out in the fresh air sometimes he would be ever so much better."

"Doesn't he ever go out?"

"No. You see, he can't walk at all, and he's too heavy to carry far. It's awfully hard for him never to see anything but chimneys. Our apartment is in the rear, so he can't even see the trolley cars."

"Why don't you take him for a drive sometimes?" Winifred asked sympathetically.

Betty's eyes sparkled.

"That's just what I'm going to do," she said triumphantly. "I never thought of it till to-day, but first the woman at the baker's spoke of it, and then Jack said he wished he could see Central Park. The day after to-morrow will be his birthday, and I'm going to hire a carriage and take him for a nice drive. I'm going to pay for it out of my own money too; it's to be my birthday present."

"That will be nice," said Winifred in a tone of satisfaction. "Does he know about it?"

"Yes, and he's so pleased. I'm going right over to the livery stable now to ask how much it will cost. It couldn't be more than a dollar, do you think it could?"

Winifred, whose ideas on the subject were quite as vague as Betty's own, and to whom a dollar appeared a rather large sum, replied that she was sure it couldn't, and after a little more conversation Betty departed on her errand.

With a beating heart the little girl crossed the street and entered the office of the livery stable on the opposite corner. A man was writing at a desk, but he looked up at her entrance, and laid down his pen.

"Well, miss, what can I do for you?" he inquired politely, as Betty paused, uncertain in just what words to put her request. "Do you want a cab?"

"No, thank you," said Betty, "at least not to-day, but I think I shall want one the day after to-morrow. Would you please tell me how much it would cost to hire a carriage to take us to Central Park?"

The man glanced at a big book which lay open on the desk before him.

"Central Park," he repeated, beginning to turn over the pages, "that would mean an afternoon drive, of course. Our regular charge for an afternoon drive is five dollars."

"Five dollars!" Betty gave a little gasp. "I didn't know it would be so expensive," she said, and without another word she turned and walked quickly out of the office.

But once outside she did not hurry. Very slowly she recrossed the street, entered at the familiar door, and began climbing the long flights of stairs. At the top of the first flight she was stopped by her new friend Winifred.

"I was watching for you," Winifred explained; "I wanted to know if it was all right about the carriage. Oh, what's the matter? Didn't you get it, after all?"

Betty shook her head; she could not speak just then, but all the bright look of pride and happiness had gone out of her face.

"Oh, I'm so sorry," said Winifred sympathetically. "Were the carriages all engaged for the day after to-morrow? Perhaps you could get one at some other stable."

"It isn't that," said Betty, trying hard to steady the quiver in her voice, "but—but they were very expensive—much more expensive than I thought. We couldn't possibly have one."

"How much are they?" Winifred inquired with interest.

"Five dollars, the man said."

"Oh!" and Winifred's eyes opened wide in astonishment; "that is a great deal of money. Uncle Will gave me a five-dollar gold-piece for Easter, and we thought it was very good of him. But if your little brother wants to go so very much, and if it's his birthday, don't you think your mother might possibly let you have the money?"

But Betty shook her head decidedly. "She couldn't possibly," she said, "I know she couldn't." And then all at once her forced composure gave way, and she burst into tears.

"Oh, he'll be so disappointed, so dreadfully disappointed," she sobbed. "Oh, I wish I had never said anything about it to him, but I was so sure a dollar would be enough, and I promised him—I promised him."

It was some few minutes later when Betty, still with red eyes, but otherwise looking much as usual, reached the top landing and paused for a moment outside their own door. Jack was so happy; how could she tell him that their cherished plan must be given up? She gave a long sigh, and drawing the door-key from her pocket, was in the act of fitting it in the lock when she heard the sound of footsteps and rustling skirts just behind her, and, turning in surprise, caught sight of a rather stout, florid lady coming up the stairs.

"This is the top floor, isn't it?" the stranger inquired rather breathlessly, as she reached the landing. She was not accustomed to climbing stairs, and did not enjoy it.

"Yes," said Betty politely.

"Well, I'm thankful to hear it, I'm sure. I never had such a climb in my life. It's an outrage not to have elevators in these high buildings. Can you tell me which is Mrs. Randall's apartment?"

"It's this one," said Betty, looking very much surprised, for she was sure she had never seen the lady before, "but Mrs. Randall is out. I'm her little girl; I could take any message."

The lady drew a step back, and stood regarding Betty with keen, though kindly scrutiny.

"So you are Mrs. Randall's little girl," she said; "I remember she told me she had children. Well, I suppose I shall have to leave my message with you, though I am sorry not to see her myself, if only to say good-bye."

"Won't you come in?" said Betty. "Mother will be at home pretty soon, I think; she generally gets back by four."

"Oh, no, I couldn't possibly spare the time; my carriage is waiting, and I have no end of things to attend to this afternoon. Will you tell your mother that Mrs. Martin called? Mrs. Henry Martin. Perhaps you may have heard her speak of me."

"Oh, yes," said Betty eagerly; "mother gives music lessons to your two little boys."

"Yes, to be sure she does, and that is the very thing I wanted to see her about. My husband has suddenly decided to go to Europe on business, and we are all going with him. It was arranged only last evening, and we sail next Saturday. I hate to take the children off like this right in the middle of the quarter, and that is why I wanted to come and see your mother about it rather than write her a note. It really can't be helped, and I know she will understand. Ask her, please, to let me have her bill, and she needn't trouble to come again; the children will be too busy to take any more lessons before we sail."

"I'll tell mother," said Betty; "she'll be sorry not to have seen you herself."

Mrs. Martin was turning away, but she glanced once more at Betty's pale little face, and then, as if with a sudden thought, she paused and drew out her purse.

"My little boys are very fond of your mother," she said kindly. "They mind her better than they ever minded any other teacher they had, and their father and I are both much pleased with her methods. I hope that another winter—but one never knows what may happen. Here's a little present for you, dear; buy something nice for yourself with it."

As she spoke, Mrs. Martin held out her hand, and in it there was a bill. Betty saw it distinctly; a crisp, new five-dollar bill.

For one breathless, delicious moment, the little girl wavered, while her heart beat so fast that she could scarcely breathe, and all the blood in her body seemed to come surging up into her face and neck. Impulsively, she held out her hand. Another second and her fingers would have closed upon the tempting gift. Suddenly her hand dropped to her side, and all the color died out of her face again, leaving it even paler than before.

"You are very kind," she said in a low, unsteady voice; "thank you very much, but—but mother doesn't like to have us take money."

Mrs. Martin looked surprised, even a little annoyed. For a moment she seemed inclined to dispute the point, but seeing the child's evident embarrassment and distress, changed her mind.

"Very well, dear," she said good-naturedly. "I am sorry you won't take my present, but you are right not to do anything of which your mother would disapprove. When we come back next autumn you must get your mother to bring you to see us some time. Now good-bye. You won't forget my message, will you?"

Jack was watching anxiously for his sister's return. At the familiar sound of the latch-key he raised himself on his elbow, straining his eyes for the first glimpse of Betty's face.

"Well, is it all right?" he cried eagerly; "are we going to have the carriage? Oh, Betty, it isn't; I see it in your eyes."

Betty said nothing, but going over to the sofa, sat down beside her little brother, slipping her arm lovingly about him. Jack winked hard and bit his lip, but he, too, was silent after that first exclamation. Perhaps even Betty herself did not realize how keen this disappointment was to the little cripple. In a few moments Betty spoke.

"It was five dollars," she said.

"Five dollars!" repeated Jack incredulously. "Oh, Betty, what a lot of money! Mother could never spare all that at once."

"I could have had it, though," said Betty, speaking fast and nervously. "I could have had every bit of it. A lady was coming to see mother; I met her on the stairs. Mother gives her little boys music lessons, and she came to say they are all going to Europe next week. She was very kind; she said she wanted to give me a present, and she offered me a five-dollar bill."

Jack gasped, and two red spots glowed in his cheeks.

"You didn't take it, did you?"

"I wanted to," said Betty slowly; "I wanted to very much. I was just going to take it in my hand, and then I remembered how mother would feel, and I didn't."

Jack heaved a deep sigh.

"I'm glad you didn't," he said rather tremulously.

Again there was silence. Both children were trying hard to keep back the coming tears. Again Betty was the first to speak.

"I suppose some mothers wouldn't mind their children taking presents," she said. "I wonder why mother is so very particular?"

"Why, don't you know?" Jack's blue eyes opened wide in surprise. "It's because we're English, and mother once lived in that beautiful place with the park and the deer. She can't forget about it, even if she is poor now. She has to remember she's a lady, and ladies never do take money from strangers."

Betty sighed impatiently.

"I suppose it's wrong," she said, "but sometimes I can't help wishing mother hadn't been quite such a grand person when she lived in England. What's the use of it now when we have to live in a flat, and mother has to give music lessons and do all the housework herself? If she hadn't had all those beautiful things once, she wouldn't mind so much about being poor now."

"Well, but it's nice to have the other things to think about," said Jack. "Aren't you glad you've got ancestors?"

"I don't think I care very much," said practical Betty; "I'd rather have relations that are alive now. Winifred Hamilton said her uncle gave her a five-dollar gold-piece for Easter. I wish we had an uncle, don't you?"

"We have got Uncle Jack," said Jack thoughtfully, "but we don't know where he is, and mother doesn't like to have us ask her about him. There's the door bell, and it's mother's ring. Wait one minute, Betty, please. Don't say anything to her about the carriage; she'd be so sorry to think we were disappointed, you know."

"No, I won't," said Betty emphatically.

CHAPTER III

WINIFRED'S THANK OFFERING

"Mother, dear, I want to talk to you about something very important."

"Well, my pet, what is it?" And Mrs. Hamilton laid aside her book, and took her little daughter into her lap.

It was the hour before dinner; the time of day that Winifred always liked best, because then her mother was never busy, and was quite ready to tell her stories, play games, or discuss any subject under the sun.

"It's about a story I've been reading," said Winifred, nestling her head comfortably on her mother's shoulder. "It's a lovely story, all about a little boy who was stolen and had to act in a circus and live in a caravan. He had a very hard time, but in the end his father and mother found him, and they were so happy that his father built a hospital for poor children just to show how grateful he was. He called it a Thank Offering."

Winifred paused to give a long, contented glance about the pretty, comfortable room. Her mother softly stroked the fluffy little head resting against her shoulder. She knew there was more to come.

"Well," Winifred went on after a moment, "I've been thinking a great deal about that story. You see, I think I feel very much the way those people did. Since you and father came home from California, and we came here to live, I've been so very, very happy. I say a little prayer to God about it sometimes, but I think I should like to do something for a Thank Offering too."

"What would you like to do?" Mrs. Hamilton asked, stooping to kiss the sweet, earnest little face.

"Well, I've been thinking about that, and it seems as if the best thing would be to make some one else very happy. You know the five-dollar gold-piece that Uncle Will gave me for Easter?"

"Yes, dear."

"Well, do you think he would mind very much if I spent it all on giving somebody else a good time?"

"He would not mind in the least, I am sure, but I thought you had decided to buy a bracelet just like Lulu Bell's."

"Yes, I had; but, you see, that was before I began to think about the Thank Offering."

"Well, and when did you first begin to think of the Thank Offering?" Mrs. Hamilton asked, smiling.

"It was yesterday afternoon, when Betty Randall was so disappointed because the man at the livery stable told her it would cost five dollars for a carriage to take her little brother for a drive. I've been thinking about it ever since, and to-day at recess I told Lulu, and she thinks just the same as I do."

"You mean that you would like to spend your five dollars in hiring a carriage to take that little cripple boy and his sister for a drive?"

"Yes, mother; do you think I might? I don't know the little boy yet, but I like Betty very much, and she was so disappointed."

Mrs. Hamilton was looking both pleased and interested.

"I do think you might," she said heartily, "and, Winnie, dear, I like your idea of a Thank Offering very much indeed. I have been thinking a good deal about that poor child myself ever since what you told me yesterday. Didn't you say to-morrow would be the little boy's birthday?"

"Yes, to-morrow; and to-morrow will be Saturday too. Oh, mother, dear, do you really think we could?"

"I will go up and call on Mrs. Randall this evening," said Mrs. Hamilton with decision. "I have never met her, but I like her little girl's appearance very much. I don't believe she will have any objection to letting the children go with us. There's father's key. Run and open the door for him and give him a nice kiss."

It was about half-past eight that evening when Mrs. Hamilton left her own apartment and climbed the three flights of stairs to the top floor. On the last landing she paused to get her breath before ringing the Randalls' bell, and at that moment her ear caught the sound of music. Some one was playing on the piano, and playing in a way that at once attracted Mrs. Hamilton's attention. This was not the kind of music she was accustomed to hearing through open windows or thin walls. Mrs. Hamilton had studied music herself under some of the best teachers the city could produce, and she knew at once that this was no ordinary musician. She had heard that Mrs. Randall gave music lessons, but she had never expected anything like this.

She stood quite still, listening until the piece came to an end, and then as the last notes of the beautiful nocturne died away, she raised her head and lightly touched the electric bell. The door was opened by the same little girl she had seen the day before.

"Good-evening," said the visitor, smiling pleasantly, "is your mother at home?"

"Yes," said Betty, looking very much surprised, but standing aside to let the lady pass; "she's in the parlor playing to Jack."

Mrs. Hamilton crossed the narrow hall, and entered the small but very neat-looking parlor. She noticed at a glance the plants in the window; the canary in his gilt cage, and the little crippled boy lying on the sofa. Jack's face was flushed with pleasure, and his blue eyes, full of sweet content, rested lovingly on the figure of the lady at the piano. At the sight of the unexpected visitor the lady rose.

"Mother," said Betty eagerly, "it's Mrs. Hamilton—Winifred Hamilton's mother."

A slight flush rose in Mrs. Randall's cheeks, but her greeting, though perhaps a little formal, was perfectly courteous. Mrs. Hamilton saw at a glance that the woman at the baker's had not exaggerated when she had described Betty's mother as "a very handsome lady." She was very tall and stately, and she spoke in a low, refined voice. Her eyes were large and dark, and there was a look in them that seemed to tell of suffering—a look that went straight to Mrs. Hamilton's kind heart.

It was impossible for any one to remain long ill at ease in the society of sweet, genial Mrs. Hamilton, and in five minutes the two ladies were chatting pleasantly together, and Mrs. Randall had almost ceased to wonder why her neighbor should have intruded upon her at this unseasonable hour. Mrs. Hamilton made friends with Jack in a way that won his heart at once, and Betty sat watching her with frank admiration. At last the visitor said:

"And now I must really explain my reason for troubling you at this time of the evening, Mrs. Randall. My little Winifred has taken a great fancy to your Betty, and is most anxious to make the acquaintance of Jack as well. She and I are going for a drive in the park to-morrow afternoon, and I have come to ask you if you will allow Betty and Jack to go with us."

The color deepened in Mrs. Randall's face, and she began to be a little formal again.

"You are very kind," she began politely, "but I am afraid——"

A low exclamation from both children checked the words on her lips, and she glanced anxiously from one eager little face to the other. Betty was actually pale with suppressed excitement, and Jack's blue eyes said unutterable things.

"You needn't be afraid to trust Jack to us," Mrs. Hamilton went on, just as if she had not heard her hostess's courteous words; "the janitor can carry him up and down stairs, and I promise to take the very best care of him."

"You are very kind," Mrs. Randall said again, and this time there was more warmth in her tone. "The children would enjoy it immensely, I know. You would like to go, wouldn't you, Jack, darling?"

"Like it! Oh, mother, I should love it better than anything in the world."

Of course there was no more hesitation after that, and when Mrs. Hamilton went downstairs ten minutes later, it was to tell Winifred the good news that Mrs. Randall had given her consent, and that the carriage was to be ordered for three o'clock the following afternoon.

"I rather like Mrs. Randall," Mrs. Hamilton said to her husband when Winifred had slipped away to her room, to tell her children all about her Thank Offering; "she is a lady, one can see that at once, and, oh, Phil, she was playing the piano when I went upstairs. I haven't heard such music in years. I think she has seen better days, and is inclined to resent anything that seems like patronage. There is a look in her eyes that somehow made my heart ache."

Mrs. Randall was very silent for some time after her visitor had left. She closed the piano, and went away to sit by herself in her dark little bedroom, leaving the children to chatter over the delightful prospect for the morrow, and when she came back to put Jack to bed, her eyes looked as if she had been crying.

"Mother," whispered the little boy, laying his cheek softly against his mother's as she bent to give him a last good-night kiss, "you aren't sorry you said yes, are you?"

"No, darling," she answered tenderly; "I can never be sorry about anything that gives my little boy pleasure, but, oh, Jack dear, I wish I had the money to take you myself."

Betty's first action on waking the next morning was to rush to the window to ascertain the state of the weather.

"It's perfectly lovely, Jack," she announced joyfully, running from the room she shared with her mother into the tiny one Jack occupied. "The sun is shining as bright as can be, there isn't a cloud in the sky. Here's your birthday present; it's only a box of drawing pencils, but I couldn't go far enough to buy anything else yesterday, and I thought you'd like it."

Jack, who was already sitting up in bed, hugging a new story book, assured his sister that drawing pencils were the very things he most wanted.

"And see what mother gave me," he added, holding up the new book for Betty's inspection, "'The Boys of Seventy-six.' Oh, Betty, I do think birthdays are lovely things, don't you?"

That was a busy morning for the Randalls. Being Saturday, there were no lessons for Mrs. Randall to give, but there was all the weekly house-cleaning to be done, and Betty and her mother worked steadily until luncheon time. If Mrs. Randall had ancestors, she had also plenty of good common sense. She was not too proud to work for her little ones, however unwilling she might be to accept favors for them from others, and she plied broom and mop to such good purpose that by twelve o'clock the little home was the very picture of neatness and order. Jack lay on the sofa as usual, too happy in eager anticipations for the afternoon to forget them even in the interest of his new story book.

Mrs. Randall went out for a little while after luncheon, returning with a pretty blue sailor cap for Jack. The thought had suddenly occurred to Betty that her brother possessed no outdoor garments, and for a moment she was filled with dismay, but her mother assured her that, with the aid of her own long cape and the new sailor cap, the little boy would do very well indeed.

"I wish I had time to finish your new dress though, dear," she said, glancing regretfully at the darn in Betty's skirt. "I tried to do it last night, but my eyes hurt me, and I was afraid to work any longer."

"I don't mind one bit," declared Betty, remembering to have wakened in the night just as the clock was striking twelve, and found her mother's place in bed still empty. "I think this dress is nice enough, and I'm sure Mrs. Hamilton and Winifred are too kind to care about what people wear."

"I care though," said Mrs. Randall with a sigh; "I should like to have people think that my little girl was a lady."

"Well, if I behave nicely and am ladylike, won't they think so any way?" inquired Betty innocently. At which her mother smiled in spite of herself, and gave her a kiss.

At three o'clock precisely there was a ring at the door bell, and Mrs. Hamilton appeared. She was closely followed by Mr. Jones, the good-natured janitor, who lifted Jack in his strong arms and carried him downstairs as easily as if he had been a baby. Mrs. Randall accompanied the party to the sidewalk, and stood by, watching anxiously while the little cripple was placed carefully and tenderly on the seat of the comfortable carriage Mrs. Hamilton had procured. She looked so sad and wistful that kind Mrs. Hamilton longed to ask her to take her place in the carriage, but dared not, lest in doing so she might arouse her neighbor's sensitive pride.

At last all was ready, Mrs. Hamilton and the two little girls were in their places, and the carriage moved slowly away from the door.

"Good-bye, mother, dear," cried Jack, waving his thin little hand as he leaned comfortably back among his pillows; "I'm having such a lovely, lovely time."

There were tears in Mrs. Randall's dark eyes as she turned away, and when she had gone back to her own rooms, instead of at once settling down to her afternoon's sewing, she threw herself wearily upon Jack's sofa and buried her face in the pillows with a sob.

What a drive that was! I don't think any one of those four people will ever forget it.

"It was one of the loveliest experiences I ever had in my life, Phil," Mrs. Hamilton told her husband that evening with tears in her eyes. "To see that dear little fellow's wonder and delight over the very simplest things was enough to make one ashamed of ever having been dissatisfied with one's lot or discontented about anything. I never before in my life saw any one so perfectly happy."

It was pretty to see the devotion of the two little girls to the poor crippled boy.

"Are you quite sure you're comfortable, Jack?" Winifred kept asking over and over again, while Betty looked anxiously into her brother's radiant face to make sure he was not getting tired.

It was a glorious spring afternoon, and the park had never looked more lovely. How Jack enjoyed it no words could describe.

"I don't believe mother's park was any more beautiful than this one," he said to Betty, as, in answer to a direction from Mrs. Hamilton the coachman turned the horses to go round a second time. "I haven't seen any deer, but there are sheep and swans."

"Where's your mother's park?" Winifred inquired, with pardonable curiosity.

Betty blushed and gave her brother a warning glance. Jack looked as if he had said something he was sorry for.

"It's a story mother tells us," he explained, "about a park she used to see when she lived in England. It was a beautiful park, and we love to hear about it."

"My friend Lulu Bell's father and mother used to live in England," said Winifred, "and she went there with them once for a visit. Did you ever live there?"

"No," answered Betty, Jack's attention having been called off for the moment by the sight of some new wonder, "father and mother came to this country before we were born."

"Has your father been long dead, dear?" Mrs. Hamilton asked kindly.

"He died six years ago, when I was only five. I don't remember him very well, and Jack doesn't remember him at all. Oh, Jack, look at that carriage without any horses. That's an automobile."

It was nearly five o'clock before the carriage again drew up before the door of the big apartment house, and Mr. Jones came out and once more lifted Jack in his arms to carry him upstairs.

There was a tinge of bright color on the little boy's usually pale cheeks and his eyes were shining.

"I've had the most beautiful time I ever had in my life," he said, turning to Mrs. Hamilton with a radiant smile. "You've been so very kind, and so has Winifred, and—and, please, I'd like to kiss you both."

CHAPTER IV

GATHERING CLOUDS

"Oh, dear! I do wish it would stop raining," sighed Betty, glancing out of the window one wet afternoon a few days later. "It's rained just as hard as it can for two whole days, and it doesn't look a bit more like clearing now than it did yesterday morning."

"I hope mother won't take any more cold," said Jack, rather anxiously, pausing in his task of endeavoring to draw a sketch from memory of an automobile. "She coughed dreadfully last night; it woke me up. I wish she didn't have to go out on rainy days."

"So do I," said Betty decidedly. "Don't you hate being poor, Jack?"

"If you were only grown up," Jack went on, ignoring his sister's question, "you could go out and give the lessons on wet days or when mother didn't feel well, and she could stay at home and rest."

"No, I couldn't," said Betty, dolefully. "You know I'm not a bit musical; I couldn't play like mother if I tried all my life. I don't see how I'm ever going to be any kind of a teacher if I can't go to school and get a diploma. People can't teach without diplomas; Mrs. Flynn says so. Her daughter's trying for one this year."

"Well, you would be able to do something any way," Jack maintained, "and mother wouldn't have to work so dreadfully hard. I wish you were grown up, Betty, only then I should have to be grown up too, and I shouldn't like that."

"Why not?" inquired Betty in some surprise.

Jack flushed, and turned his face towards the wall.

"I don't know exactly," he stammered, "but I think—I'm sure it must be much worse to be a grown up cripple, than to be a little boy one."

Betty left her seat by the window, and coming over to her brother's side, sat down on the end of the sofa by Jack's feet.

"You wouldn't mind so much if you could be a great artist and paint beautiful pictures, would you, Jack?" she asked gently.

"N—no, I don't suppose I should, not quite so much, because then I could sell my pictures, and make lots of money for you and mother. Then we could live in a lovely place in the country, and keep a carriage."

"And you could go to drive every day," added Betty, falling in at once with Jack's fancy, "and mother could have a fine piano, and go to hear all the concerts and operas. Then we could give money to poor people instead of having people want to give it to us, and I could be very accomplished, and go to parties sometimes."

"Yes," said Jack eagerly, "and some time we could all go to England, and see the place where mother used to live."

Betty looked a little doubtful.

"I don't know whether mother would like that or not," she said. "You see, when mother lived there she knew father, and now he's dead. It might make her feel badly to go back."

"So it might; I never thought about that, but she might like to see Uncle Jack. I should like to see him, shouldn't you, Betty?"

"Yes; I wonder if we ever shall. Mother doesn't like to have us talk much about him, but I know she loves him very much; her eyes always look that way when she tells us how handsome and splendid he used to be when he was a boy."

"Wouldn't it be nice if Winifred Hamilton came to see us this afternoon," Jack remarked rather irrelevantly; "I do like her very much, don't you?"

"Yes, she's lovely; she said she'd come to see you some day."

"We haven't seen her since the day we went for the drive. Perhaps she's waiting for you to call on her first."

"Mother won't let me go," said Betty regretfully; "she says she's afraid Mrs. Hamilton might not want Winifred to know us."

"But if she hadn't wanted to know us she wouldn't have taken us to drive, would she?"

"I shouldn't think so, but, any way, mother won't let me go there till Winifred has been here."

"There's the clock striking four," exclaimed Jack joyfully; "mother'll be in in a few minutes now. Why don't you light the gas stove, Betty, and get her slippers nice and warm? She'll be so tired and wet."

"I will," said Betty, springing up with alacrity; "and I'll make her a cup of tea, too; she'll like that." And away bustled the little housewife, disappointment and vexation alike forgotten in the pleasant prospect of making mother comfortable.

She had scarcely finished her preparations, and the kettle was just beginning to boil, when the familiar ring was heard, and she flew to open the door.

Jack was quite correct in his predictions; Mrs. Randall was both wet and tired. Indeed, she came in looking so much more tired than usual that Betty noticed it, and inquired anxiously as she hung up the dripping umbrella, and helped her mother off with her waterproof, "Have you got a headache, mother, dear?"

"Yes, dear, I have a bad headache. My cold is rather bad, too; I have been coughing a great deal to-day. Is Jack all right?"

"Oh, yes; he ate a good lunch, and was reading all the morning, and drawing pictures all the afternoon."

"How chilly it feels here," Mrs. Randall said, shivering and coughing as she spoke.

"I've lighted the stove, and your slippers are nice and warm," said Betty proudly. "The kettle's boiling too, and I'll have a nice cup of tea for you in five minutes."

Mrs. Randall's tired face brightened, and she looked rather relieved.

"That is good," she said. "Hurry as quickly as you can with the tea, dear, for I believe I am really chilled through."

Betty, nothing loath, flew about like a small whirlwind; had her mother's wet shoes off and the warm slippers in their place; drew the comfortable armchair as near as possible to the steam radiator, and darted away to the kitchen, from whence she returned in a twinkling, with a cup of steaming tea.

Mrs. Randall drank the tea, but though she pronounced it delicious, and declared herself ever so much better, she still shivered, and cowered over the radiator for warmth. Jack watched her anxiously, with a troubled look on his pale little face.

In a little while Mrs. Randall rose.

"I think I will go and lie down," she said, and the children noticed that her voice was very hoarse. "My head is bad, and if I could sleep for half an hour I might be all right. Be sure and call me in time to get dinner, Betty."

"I hope mother isn't going to be ill," said Jack anxiously, when they were once more alone together.

"Oh, I guess not," said cheerful Betty; "she's only got a cold and a headache. She'll be better after she's rested. Let's play a game of lotto."

Jack assented, but though they played several games, and Betty did her best to be entertaining, the troubled expression did not leave his face. Suddenly he stopped short in the middle of a game.

"Hear mother coughing, Betty; she can't be asleep. I wish you'd go and see if she wants anything."

Betty rose promptly, and hurried into the little bedroom. Her mother was lying on her bed, with flushed cheeks and wide-open eyes. At sight of her little girl she smiled faintly.

"I'm getting nice and warm now, dear," she said; "that tea did me so much good. I'm going to get up very soon."

"You look ever so much better," said Betty in a tone of decided relief. "You've got a lovely color in your cheeks."

Mrs. Randall pressed her hand to her forehead, but said nothing, and next moment a violent spasm of coughing shook her from head to foot.

The evening that followed was a decidedly uncomfortable one. Mrs. Randall's cough was very painful, and although she went about as usual, and tried to appear like herself, it was easy to see that every movement cost her an effort. Betty noticed that she scarcely tasted any dinner, and Jack's eyes never left her face. Almost as soon as dinner was over Jack said he was tired, and would like to go to bed. The others soon followed, and by nine o'clock the lights were out, and the little family settled for the night.

But there was little sleep for at least two members of the household. Mrs. Randall coughed incessantly, and tossed from side to side in feverish restlessness. Betty lay with wide-open eyes, and a heavier heart than she had ever known before. It was all very well to assure Jack that there was not much the matter with mother, and that she would surely be all right in the morning. She knew nothing about illness, but she could not help thinking that that dreadful cough and those burning hands meant something more than an every-day cold.

"I am afraid I am disturbing you very much, dear," Mrs. Randall said at last, when the clock struck ten, and a restless movement on Betty's part assured her that the child was still wide awake. "I wish I could be quieter, but this cough——"

"Never mind, mother, I'm not one bit sleepy. I'm really not. Wouldn't you like to have me get you some water or something?"

"No, thank you, darling; I'm afraid it wouldn't do any good, but if you are not asleep I should like to talk to you a little."

Betty took one of the hot hands in both her little cool ones, and patted it gently. After another fit of coughing, her mother went on.

"You are only a little girl, Betty, but you are very sensible, and in many ways seem older than you really are. There are some things that I think you ought to know about, in case anything should ever happen to me."

"But nothing is going to happen, is it, mother?" Betty asked in a rather frightened whisper. They both spoke in whispers, so as not to disturb Jack in the next room.

"No, no, dear, of course not; I only said 'in case.' I am sure I shall be all right in the morning, but if at any time I should be ill, Betty—if anything serious were to happen to me—you and Jack would be all alone."

Betty nestled closer to her mother's side, and softly kissed the hot fingers.

"I sometimes fear, dear, that I have done wrong in not making more friends," Mrs. Randall said, after another fit of coughing. "People would have been kind I dare say, but I have always been so proud and reserved. Some of the families where I teach would have been friendly if I had let them. I almost wish now that I had."

"Mrs. Hamilton is very kind," said Betty eagerly; "and she came to see you."

"Yes, dear, and I liked her too, but I have always so dreaded being patronized. You know, dear, that I haven't always been poor."

"Yes, mother, I know; you were not poor in England."

"I have often told you about my English home, and about your Uncle Jack, and how happy we were together when we were children. I have been thinking a great deal of those times this evening, and all last night I dreamed of Jack."

"He was your twin brother, wasn't he, mother?"

"Yes; and we were everything to each other. Our mother died when we were babies, and our two sisters were much older, almost grown up in fact, while we were still little children. I suppose my father loved us in his way, but he was very stern, and we were all rather afraid of him. Our older sisters were very good to us little ones, but they had their own affairs to think of, and so Jack and I were left a good deal to ourselves. Such merry times as we had—such pranks as we played."

"You mean the time when Uncle Jack rode the wild colt, and the day you climbed the plum tree, and fell and broke your arm," said Betty, glad to have her mother's thoughts turn in this direction, and hopeful of new stories.

"Yes, those and many others, but, Betty dear, I want to talk to you about something else to-night. You have never heard very much about your father, have you, darling?"

"No, mother," said Betty softly; "I know you don't like to talk about him."

"I ought to like it, but I loved him so dearly that for a long time after his death I could not bring myself to mention his name to any one, even my own children."

"Did Uncle Jack love him too?" Betty asked rather timidly; "you said you always liked the same things."

"They never met. Jack was at college when your father first came into our neighborhood. He came to visit at the vicarage; Mr. Marvyn, our vicar, had known his father. By that time both my sisters were married, and as I was often lonely at home when Jack was away, I got into the habit of spending a good many days with the Marvyn girls, who were about my own age. Your father was only a poor artist, but he was very clever, and people said he would make his mark in the world some day. Jack was very fond of sketching himself, and I think that was one reason why I first began to be interested in your father. We used to go off on sketching expeditions together that spring, and we grew to know each other very well. Jack was invited to spend his summer vacation in Switzerland with a party of friends, and he decided to go. It was the first vacation he had not spent with me, and I think I was more hurt and jealous than I had any right to be under the circumstances. I wrote him how I felt, and he, as was only natural, thought me silly, and told me so. That made me angry, and we quarreled for the first time in our lives. It was only a foolish little quarrel, but it kept me from telling him, as I should otherwise have done, how much I was going about with Archie Randall.

"At first my father did not seem to notice how things were going, but I think some one must have warned him, for one day when I came back from a long walk with your father, he called me into his study, and told me he did not wish me to have anything more to do with young Randall, who was only a penniless artist, and not a proper companion for one of his daughters.

"I am not going to tell you about that time, Betty. I was very angry, and I am afraid I did not behave very well towards my father, who was an old man, and who I think really loved me. When he found that I would not obey him, he sent for Archie, and forbade him to see me again. Then all at once your father and I found out how much we cared for each other. He was very honorable. He wanted me to wait for him while he went away and made a name for himself, but I was young and headstrong, and I loved him better than anything else in the world. The end of it was that we ran away, and were married in London by special license."

Betty gasped. This was the most interesting, romantic story she had ever heard.

"And didn't your father ever forgive you?" she questioned breathlessly.

"No, never. He wrote me one letter after my marriage, and only one. He said that I had disgraced my family, and he never wished to see my face again. He said he had changed his will, and that neither I nor my husband should ever inherit a penny of his money."

"And Uncle Jack, was he angry too?"

"He wrote me only once. He was very much grieved, and could not understand how I could have acted as I had done. That was twelve years ago and I have never heard a word from him since.

"We came to America, and after a time your father obtained employment as an illustrator for a publishing firm here in New York. Then you and Jack were born. We were very happy in those days, and if it had not been for my longing to see Jack and know that he forgave me, I should have been quite content. I was too proud to write to him, but kept hoping that something would happen to bring us together again, and that he and my husband might become good friends. Then, six years ago, just as we were beginning to feel that we were really making our way in the world, your father died."

Mrs. Randall paused, and Betty felt the hand she held quiver convulsively, but after a moment's pause she went on again.

"It was a terrible struggle at first. I had never been brought up to support myself, and now I was left alone in the world with two little helpless children to care for. Little Jack was frightfully delicate. The doctors told me that it was only by the very tenderest care that I could hope to save him. Twice I decided to write to my brother Jack. He would help me, I knew. I even wrote the letters, but I tore them up again. I was too proud. I could not ask for help even from him.

"My music was my only talent, and in time I succeeded in procuring pupils. It has been hard work ever since, but I have managed somehow, and you and Jack have never suffered."

"No, indeed, we haven't, mother; we've had lots of good times, and Jack is ever so much stronger than he used to be."

"I know that, and I am very thankful. If I can only keep my health—I have always been very strong. Why, I don't think I have ever been really ill in my life."

A spasm of coughing interrupted Mrs. Randall's words, and it was several minutes before she was able to speak again.

"I don't know why I am telling you all this to-night, Betty, unless it is that I feel so restless and wakeful. If I keep well everything will be all right, but if anything should ever happen—things do happen sometimes you know, darling—if you and Jack are ever left alone in the world, then you must try to find your Uncle Jack. He will be good to you and love you for my sake, I know."

"Where does he live, mother?"

"I don't know where he is now, but a letter sent to the old home would probably reach him. My father has been dead for nearly two years—I saw the notice of his death in an English newspaper—and Jack, as his only son, would naturally inherit everything. My father was a general, you know—General Stanhope. In my desk you will find a letter addressed to John Stanhope, Esq., Stonybrook Grange, Devonshire, England. That is the address of my old home. You must see that it is stamped and posted. I wrote it shortly after my father's death. I thought that I ought to make some provision in case of anything happening to me. In it I have told him everything, and asked him to care for you and Jack. Why, my darling, what are you crying for? I didn't say anything was going to happen. Hush, I hear Jack stirring; I am afraid our talk is disturbing him. Now turn over like a good little girl, and go to sleep. I feel better than I did, and I shall try to go to sleep too."

Betty, much reassured by her mother's words, obeyed as far as turning over was concerned, and soon the only sounds to be heard were the ticking of the clock and Mrs. Randall's heavy breathing. Betty lay awake for some time, thinking over the story she had heard, but she was only a little girl, after all, and before very long her thoughts grew dim and confused; she fell into a doze, and in a few moments more was fast asleep.

CHAPTER V

WINIFRED TO THE RESCUE

When Betty next opened her eyes it was broad daylight, and the morning sunshine was peeping through the chinks of the shutters. Her first thought was of her mother, and she was glad to find that Mrs. Randall was still asleep. She was breathing heavily, but her eyes were closed, and she did not cough. Even when Betty rose softly, and crept round to the other side of the bed to look at her more closely, she did not move, although she was as a rule a very light sleeper.

"It's after seven," said Betty to herself, glancing rather uneasily at the clock; "I don't think mother ever slept so late before."

Just then she heard Jack stirring in his bed, and she hurried into the next room to tell him to be very quiet, as mother was still asleep.

"Is she better?" Jack inquired in an anxious whisper, as Betty bent over him in motherly fashion, to arrange his pillows more comfortably.

"Yes, I think so; her eyes are shut, and she's lying very still. I only just woke up myself."

"I've been awake for ever so long," said Jack; "I've been listening to mother. She doesn't cough so much any more, but she breathes so hard, and sometimes she moans. Oh, Betty, I'm frightened; I don't know why, but I am." And the poor little fellow buried his face in the pillow, and began to cry.

Betty dropped on her knees by the bedside, striving to comfort her little brother by every means in her power.

"There isn't anything to be frightened about, Jack, there really isn't," she whispered soothingly. "Mother's all right; she told me she was better last night before she went to sleep, and, oh, Jack dear, she told me something else; such an interesting story, all about father and our grandfather and

Uncle Jack. I'll tell you all of it by and by. There's mother calling me; don't let her see you've been crying."

Mrs. Randall's eyes were open when Betty returned to her bedside. Indeed, the little girl's first impression was that they were unusually bright. There was a bright color in her cheeks too, but Mrs. Randall's first words quickly dispelled Betty's hope that she was better.

"I'm afraid I shall not be able to get up this morning, Betty," she said, and her voice had sunk to a hoarse whisper now; "I seem to have lost all my strength, and there is such a terrible pain in my chest that I can scarcely breathe."

"Oh, mother, what shall we do?" cried Betty in sudden consternation. "Oughtn't you to have a doctor come to see you?"

Mrs. Randall shook her head decidedly.

"No, no," she said impatiently, "I can't afford to have a doctor; I will lie here for a while, and perhaps I shall feel better. What day is it?"

"Thursday," said Betty, trying to control the sudden trembling of her knees.

"That's too bad; Mrs. Flynn is always engaged on Thursdays, I know. I thought she might be able to come in and help. Well, you'll have to manage about breakfast as well as you can. I don't want anything myself, but you must prepare some oatmeal, and boil some eggs for Jack and yourself. Tell Jack he must stay in bed a little while longer, but that just as soon as I can I will come and dress him."

That was the strangest morning Betty and Jack had ever spent. Never before in their remembrance had their mother failed to be up and about by seven o'clock. Even in those sad days, which Betty could just remember, after their father's death, her own grief had never prevented her from fulfilling the little household duties. Now she lay still, with closed eyes, scarcely noticing what went on about her. Betty brought her some tea, and she drank it thirstily, but refused to touch any food. Once she roused herself sufficiently to say that she thought a mustard plaster on her chest might ease the pain, but when Betty inquired anxiously how to make one, she did not answer, and seemed to have forgotten all about the matter.

Jack was very good and patient, but he was, if anything, more frightened than Betty, and his white, drawn little face was pitiful to see. Betty made him as tidy as she could, gave him his breakfast, and brought him his new story book to read, but he shook his head mournfully.

"I don't want to read this morning," he said; "I'd rather just lie still."

"Oh, Jack, you're not going to be ill too, are you?" cried Betty, the tears starting to her eyes.

"No, I'm not ill, only I can't read; I wish I could see how mother looks."

"She looks all right," said Betty encouragingly; "she's got a lovely color in her cheeks, only I wish she'd wake up and talk about things. I don't know what to do about going to market, and I suppose we ought to tell her pupils she can't give them any lessons to-day."

"She's talking now, I hear her," said Jack in a tone of relief. "Oh, Betty, she's calling me. Yes, mother, dear, I'm all right; I'm so glad you're better."

Betty flew to her mother's side.

"Are you better, mother?" she asked eagerly. "I'm so glad you're awake, because I want to ask——" She paused abruptly, terrified by the strange look in those bright, feverish eyes. Her mother was looking straight into her face, but did not seem to see her.

"Jack, Jack," she kept repeating in her low, hoarse whisper, "Jack, I want you. I did wrong, I know, but you will forgive me. You will be good to the children, and love them for my sake, won't you, Jack?"

Betty's face was very white, her eyes big with terror.

"Jack," she gasped, running back to her brother's room, and flinging herself down beside him in an abandonment of grief and despair, "mother's talking in her sleep; she doesn't know what she's saying. She thinks Uncle Jack is here. Oh, what shall we do—what shall we do?"

"We'll have to get some one to come and see her," said Jack with decision. "Run down and ask Mrs. Hamilton to come; I know she will, she's so kind."

Betty sprang to her feet.

"I'll go right away," she said, "perhaps she'll know what to do. Mother says she can't afford to have a doctor. Oh, there's the door bell; I'm so glad somebody's come."

She ran to the door, threw it open, and then drew back a step in surprise. The visitor was Winifred Hamilton.

"Good-morning," said Winifred pleasantly. "Mother's gone out shopping with Aunt Estelle, and she said I might come and see you and Jack. I was coming before, but I've had a bad cold ever since Saturday, and mother was afraid of the draughts on the stairs. I haven't been to school all the week. Why, what's the matter—is Jack ill?"

"No," said Betty; "Jack's all right, but oh, I'm so sorry your mother's gone out. I was just going to ask her if she wouldn't please come up here to see mother."

"Is there something the matter with your mother?" Winifred inquired sympathetically.

"She had a bad cold yesterday, and this morning she's worse. She keeps her eyes shut most of the time, and doesn't understand the things I say to her. I'm afraid she is very ill—oh, I'm afraid she is." And Betty burst into tears.

Winifred's tender little heart was filled with compassion.

"Don't cry, don't," she whispered, throwing her arms impulsively around Betty's neck; "maybe she'll be all right soon. I'll tell mother about it the minute she comes in, and she'll come right up. Do you think Jack would like to have me stay with him for a while? I might read to him while you're doing things for your mother."

Betty said she was sure Jack would like it very much, and having dried her eyes on Winifred's handkerchief, she led the way to her brother's bedside.

"Jack," said Betty softly, "here's Winifred Hamilton. Her mother's out, but she's going to tell her about mother just as soon as she comes home."

Jack looked pleased.

"I'm glad to see you," he said politely, holding out his thin little hand. "I'm usually up on the sofa by this time, but mother wasn't able to dress me this morning."

"That's all right," said Winifred, giving the outstretched hand a hearty squeeze. "When people aren't very strong they often stay in bed quite late, you know. Your mother's awake now, isn't she, Betty? I hear her talking."

Betty stole on tiptoe to her mother's door, but returned in a moment.

"She's only talking in her sleep," she said anxiously. "I spoke to her, but she didn't answer. Did you ever see any one who was very ill, Winifred?"

"I saw Mr. Bradford have an attack once," said Winifred; "his eyes were shut, and he looked very white. Mrs. Bradford sent for the doctor. Why don't you have a doctor come to see your mother?"

"She doesn't want one," said Betty, coloring. "I asked her this morning, and she said she didn't. Would you mind coming to look at her, Winifred? Perhaps you can tell what the matter is."

Winifred said she would not mind, and, hand in hand, the two little girls stole into the dark little bedroom, and stood looking down at the flushed face on the pillow. Mrs. Randall was tossing restlessly from side to side, and talking in a low, incoherent way.

"Mother," said Betty in a voice that she tried hard to make steady and cheerful, "here's Winifred Hamilton. She came up to see us, and she's going to read to Jack."

Mrs. Randall muttered something unintelligible, and her eyes wandered past the two children, and fixed themselves vacantly on the opposite wall.

"I'm not going to be ill," she said, apparently addressing some unseen person; "I can't be ill, you know. I must take care of the children; there's no one else to do it."

"She's delirious," whispered Winifred, looking frightened. "I never saw any one like that before, but I've read about it in books. I'm sure a doctor ought to see her."

Betty's cheeks were scarlet, and her eyes drooped, but she said nothing, and in silence they went back to Jack. The little boy looked imploringly at

Winifred, as if with some faint hope that she might be able to set matters right.

"Do you think she's very ill?" he asked tremulously.

"I think a doctor ought to see her," said Winifred decidedly. "My friend Lulu Bell's papa is a doctor, and he's very kind. Would you like to have me ask him to come and see your mother?"

"No," said Betty sharply; "mother doesn't want a doctor; I told you so before."

"But, Betty," persisted Winifred, "she ought to have some medicine or something, and we don't know what to do for her. I know mother would send for a doctor right away if she were at home."

To Winifred's surprise, Betty suddenly put up both hands before her face, and burst into a passion of crying.

"Oh, what shall we do—what shall we do?" she sobbed, rocking herself backward and forward in her distress; "we can't have a doctor, mother said we couldn't; she said we couldn't afford it."

For a moment Winifred stood motionless, uncertain what to do or say. Jack hid his face in the bedclothes, shaking from head to foot with sobs. Next instant both Winifred's arms were around Betty's neck.

"I'll tell you what I'll do, Betty," she whispered eagerly. "I'll go and see Dr. Bell myself, and tell him all about it. He's very kind indeed. Lulu says he often goes to see poor—I mean people who can't afford to pay him, and when Lulu's kitty got run over by a trolley-car and had her leg broken, he set the leg himself, and took such good care of the kitty that she got all well again. I'll go right away; he's always at home in the morning, and I know he won't mind coming one single bit. Oh, Betty, please, please do let me."

Betty wavered, but Jack, lifting his tear-stained face from the pillow, cried imploringly:

"Yes, do go, Winifred, and, oh, please ask him to come right away. Mother must have a doctor, Betty, and it doesn't matter whether she can afford it or not."

Winifred waited to hear no more. Three minutes later she was ringing violently at her own front door bell.

"Oh, Lizzie," she cried breathlessly, as the maid opened the door, "I want you to put on your hat right away, and come with me to Dr. Bell's! Mrs. Randall is very, very ill, and Betty and Jack don't know what to do for her."

At first Lizzie seemed inclined to hesitate, but when the state of the case had been more fully explained to her, she willingly consented to leave her ironing, and she and Winifred were soon in the street hurrying towards the home of Winifred's friends.

As they approached their destination, Winifred's courage began to fail. After all, she thought, she might be doing a very bold and unheard-of thing in asking a doctor to go to see a person who had frankly stated that she could not afford to employ him. What if Dr. Bell were angry—what if he refused to go? Winifred's heart sank at the thought. Her friend Lulu would be at school she knew, but possibly her mother or aunt might be at home. Winifred decided that in that case she would tell her story to them. It would be much less formidable than appealing directly to the doctor himself. Her heart was beating very fast as they mounted Dr. Bell's front steps and when the door was opened by a small boy in brass buttons, who greeted her with a broad smile of recognition, she could scarcely summon voice enough to inquire:

"Are Mrs. Bell or Miss Warren at home, Jimmie?"

"No, Miss, they've both of 'em gone out," returned the boy, regarding her somewhat curiously. "Miss Lulu's out too; she's gone to school."

"Yes, I knew Lulu would be at school," said Winifred, "but I thought Mrs. Bell or Miss Warren might be in. I—I want to see the doctor."

"Oh, the doctor's in all right. He's got a patient just now, but you can wait in the front office."

There was no help for it then, and, with a little frightened gasp, Winifred followed the boy to the doctor's comfortable office, where she sat down on a sofa to wait until he should be disengaged. She did not have long to wait. In a few moments she heard the front door open and close. Then the door of the waiting room opened and the doctor came in.

He was a tall gentleman with a kind, pleasant face, and at sight of Winifred he came quickly forward, smiling and holding out his hand.

"Good-morning, little Miss Winnie," he said pleasantly, "and what can I do for you to-day? Nothing wrong at home, I hope."

"Oh, no, sir," said Winifred, half her fears vanishing at the sound of the doctor's kind voice; "father and mother are very well. I've had a cold, but I'm all right again now. I come—that is, I want—oh, Dr. Bell, will you please do me a very great favor?"

"Do you a favor?" the doctor repeated, still smiling, and sitting down beside her on the sofa. "Yes indeed, I will—that is, if I can. What is it?"

"It's to go and see Mrs. Randall, who lives in our apartment house," Winifred explained timidly. "She's a very nice lady, but she hasn't any money to pay a doctor with. She's very ill indeed, but she told Betty— that's her little girl, you know—not to send for a doctor, because she couldn't afford it."

The doctor looked a little puzzled.

"Perhaps she wouldn't care to see me then," he said, "if she objected to having a doctor sent for."

"Oh, yes, she would," said Winifred earnestly, "at least she wouldn't know anything about it, and Betty and Jack would be so very glad. Jack is a cripple, he can't walk at all; and, oh, it's dreadful to see him so unhappy. Mrs. Randall is really very ill. She doesn't know Betty and she keeps talking to herself the way people in books do when they're delirious.

"I said I'd come and tell you about it, and I was sure you'd come, because Lulu says you're so very kind."

The doctor smiled, but he was beginning to look really interested.

"Did your mother send you for me?" he asked.

Winifred's eyes sank.

"N—no, sir," she faltered, "mother's out shopping, and doesn't know anything about it. Perhaps I oughtn't to have come, but I didn't know what else to do, and I was so very sorry for Betty and Jack."

Winifred's lip quivered, and two big tears rolled slowly down her cheeks. The doctor patted her shoulder kindly.

"You did quite right to come," he said, "and I will go to see your friend to-day."

"Will you please go just as soon as you can?" Winifred asked eagerly.

The doctor rose and looked at his watch.

"It is half-past ten now," he said. "I have to stay in my office till eleven, and then I have one or two serious cases to see, but I will be at Mrs. Randall's as early as I possibly can."

"Now run along home, and if your mother makes any objections, tell her I said you did quite right to come, and that I am very glad you did."

"Oh, thank you, sir, thank you very much indeed," said Winifred gratefully, and the look she gave the doctor said more than any words could have done. With a sudden impulse, he bent and kissed her.

"You dear little girl," he said. And then another patient was announced, and Winifred hurried away.

CHAPTER VI

FRIENDS IN NEED

By the time Dr. Bell arrived at the apartment house Betty and Jack were no longer alone with their mother. Mrs. Hamilton had returned from her shopping expedition, and as soon as she heard the story from Winifred, had hastened upstairs to see what could be done. One glance at the flushed face and bright burning eyes, had been enough to convince her that Winifred had not exaggerated matters and that Mrs. Randall was indeed very ill. As for Betty, at the first glimpse of Mrs. Hamilton's kind, sweet face it had seemed to the little girl as though a great load had been suddenly lifted from her shoulders.

Mrs. Hamilton did not waste much time in words, but at once set about the task of making everybody more comfortable. In an incredibly short time Mrs. Randall's face and hands were bathed, and her bed smoothed; Jack was dressed in his wrapper, and carried to his usual place on the sitting-room sofa, and a substantial meal was in preparation in the kitchen. When the doctor came, Mrs. Hamilton sent Betty to stay with Jack, and the two children sat silently, hand in hand, listening for any sounds that might come from their mother's room.

"Do you think the doctor will make her well right away, Betty?" Jack whispered at last.

"I guess he will if he can. He's got a very kind face, and he smiled at me when I opened the door. Hark, they're coming out now."

Next moment Mrs. Hamilton and the doctor came into the room together. They both looked grave and anxious.

"She must have a nurse," Betty heard the doctor say in a low voice. "I will send one as soon as I can, and be in again myself this evening. You will stay with her till the nurse arrives?"

"Oh, yes, certainly; and the children, what of them?"

The doctor glanced for the first time towards the sofa where the two children sat, Jack propped up with pillows, and Betty close beside him, holding his hand. He remembered what Winifred had said about the little crippled boy, and his face softened.

"We must see about them by and by," he said, "and in the meantime I think we can count on their keeping quiet."

"Oh, yes, sir," said Betty eagerly; "Jack is always very quiet indeed, and I won't make any noise."

"That's right. You are both going to be brave little people, I know, and perhaps by and by you may like to go and make a little visit to some of your friends, just until your mother gets stronger."

"We haven't any friends," said Betty; "we don't know any one at all, except Mrs. Hamilton and Winifred."

The doctor looked surprised, and a little troubled.

"No friends?" he repeated; "no aunts or cousins?"

Betty shook her head.

"We have an uncle in England," she said, "but we've never seen him. We haven't any relations in this country. Mother has her pupils, but we don't know any of them."

The doctor said no more, and was turning to leave the room, when Jack spoke for the first time since his entrance.

"Please, sir," he said tremulously, "would you mind telling us—is mother going to be well again pretty soon?"

"Pretty soon I hope, my boy," said the doctor kindly, and coming over to the sofa, he took the thin little hand in his and looked long and earnestly into Jack's troubled face. "I shall do all I can to make her well soon, you may be sure of that."

"Thank you, sir," said Jack gratefully. "I think you are a very kind gentleman," he added in his quaint, old-fashioned little way.

The doctor smiled, gave the small hand a friendly shake and hurried away, followed by Mrs. Hamilton.

That was about the longest afternoon Betty and Jack had ever known. Mrs. Hamilton was very kind, but she was too busy to pay much attention to them, and they were left pretty much to themselves. There was no use in trying to read or to play games. They tried lotto, but it proved a miserable failure. Then Betty tried reading aloud, but a big lump kept rising in her throat and choking her, and they soon gave that up as well. After all, the most comforting thing seemed to sit hand in hand, talking in whispers, and listening to every sound from the sick-room.

At about four o'clock there was a ring at the bell, and Betty, hurrying to admit the visitor, encountered in the hall a tall young woman, with a bright, sensible face, who carried a traveling bag, and who Mrs. Hamilton told her was the nurse Dr. Bell had promised to send. After that there was a good deal of whispering and moving about, but no one came near the children, and the time seemed very long indeed.

It was nearly dark when the doctor came again. The children heard his voice in the hall, and after a little while he and Mrs. Hamilton came into the sitting room together, and Mrs. Hamilton lighted the gas.

"You poor little things," she said cheerfully, "what a long, lonely afternoon you have had. They've been as quiet as little mice, doctor, and I feel sure Betty is going to be a great help to Miss Clark. As for Jack, he is going to be a good, brave little boy, and let Winifred and me take care of him till his mother gets well again."

She bent over the sofa as she spoke, and softly kissed Jack's forehead. He looked up in her face rather apprehensively, and his lip trembled.

"You're very kind indeed," he said politely, "but if you please, I'd rather stay with mother. I'll be very good."

"I know you will be good, dear; but, you see, there isn't very much room here. Betty will have to sleep in your bed, and then there is Miss Clark, you know. So I want you to be a very good boy, and come home with me. Betty shall come down to see you the first thing in the morning, and you and Winifred will have such good times together."

Jack began to cry. "I'd rather not, indeed, I would much rather not," he sobbed; "I've never been away from mother and Betty at night. Mother always puts me to bed."

Mrs. Hamilton looked distressed and rather helpless, but the doctor came to the rescue.

"Jack," he said pleasantly, sitting down beside the little boy, "what would you like to be when you grow up?"

"An artist," said Jack promptly, and in his surprise at the question he forgot to cry. "My father was an artist, and I want to be one too. My grandfather was a general, and I'd like to be a soldier, but I couldn't, you know, on account of not being able to walk."

"I don't know about that," said the doctor, smiling; "fighting isn't the only part of a soldier's duty, you know. Wouldn't you like to begin by being a brave little soldier boy now?"

"How could I?" Jack inquired wonderingly.

"Well, one very important part of a soldier's duty is to obey orders. Now we know that you want to stay here with your mother and Betty, but we feel that it will be much better for you to go home with Mrs. Hamilton, who has very kindly offered to take you with her. Betty can be a great help to Miss Clark, the nurse, if she stays here. You would like to do something to help your mother get well, wouldn't you?"

"Yes, of course I would," said Jack, with a brightening face.

"Well, the very best thing you can possibly do for her at this moment is to obey Mrs. Hamilton, and let me carry you downstairs to her rooms."

Jack was silent for a moment; his face was twitching, and he clasped and unclasped his hands nervously. Then he looked up into the doctor's face.

"All right," he said bravely, "I'll go, only—only, may I kiss mother good-night first?"

"Your mother is asleep now, but you may look at her if you like. She is more comfortable than she was this morning. Shall I take you in to have a peep at her?"

Jack nodded—he was finding it rather hard work to speak just then—and the doctor lifted him in his arms and carried him into the bedroom.

Mrs. Randall was lying with closed eyes, still breathing heavily, but no longer talking in that strange, incoherent way that had frightened Betty so much in the morning. Miss Clark, in her nurse's uniform, sat at the foot of the bed.

"Good-night, mother," Jack whispered very softly, and he kissed his hand to the motionless figure on the bed. "I'll be a good boy. Good-night and pleasant dreams."

The nurse rose, and, at a sign from Dr. Bell, followed them out of the room.

"This is Miss Clark, Jack," the doctor said; "she is taking splendid care of your mother."

"Thank you very much," said Jack, trying to smile. "Won't you please be a little kind to Betty too? I think she'll miss me."

"That I will, dear," said the nurse heartily; and then she turned away hurriedly with a suspicious moisture in her eyes.

It cost Betty a great effort to see her little brother carried away from her, and she clung to him passionately for a moment, feeling half inclined to protest against such a strange state of affairs. But she was a sensible little woman, and realizing the necessity in this case, she forced a smile, and the last words that Jack heard as the doctor carried him downstairs were Betty's cheerful assurances that she should take good care of mother, and come to see him the very first thing in the morning.

It was no easy task for Jack to keep back the tears, but he did keep them back, though he had to bite his lip and to wink very hard indeed in order to do it. Dr. Bell did not fail to notice the effort, and he found himself beginning to like this small boy immensely.

Winifred was watching for them at the open door, and she gave Jack such a rapturous greeting that it would have been impossible not to feel gratified by it. Almost before he realized what had happened, Jack found himself settled on a comfortable sofa, with Winifred hovering over him, and Mrs. Hamilton and Lizzie bustling about completing the arrangements for his comfort.

"And now I must say good-night, my little soldier," Dr. Bell said, taking Jack's hand as he spoke. "I shall come to see your mother again in the morning, and I have an idea that you and I are going to be great friends. By the way, how long is it that you have been laid up like this?"

"Ever since I was a baby," said Jack. "My nurse let me fall, and it hurt my back."

The doctor said nothing, but looked interested, and when he followed Mrs. Hamilton out of the room a few moments later he asked her how long she had known the Randall family.

"I never spoke to them until last week," said Mrs. Hamilton, and in a few words she told the story of Winifred's Thank Offering. The doctor looked considerably surprised.

"Do you mean to tell me that they are almost total strangers to you, and yet that you are willing to take all this trouble for them?"

Mrs. Hamilton smiled.

"People learn to help each other where I have lived," she said simply; "and besides, I am so happy myself now that I think I feel a little as Winifred does, and should like to make a Thank Offering too."

"I wish there were more people in the world like you and Winifred," said the doctor heartily. "I am sure it would be a better place than it is if there were."

An hour later Jack was lying in a soft bed in the little room opening out of Winifred's. Mrs. Hamilton had undressed him almost as tenderly as his mother could have done; had heard him say his prayers, and when at last she had bent down to give him a good-night kiss, Jack's warm little heart had overflowed, and he had suddenly thrown his arms around her neck.

"I love you," he whispered softly; "oh, I do love you very much."

But when Mrs. Hamilton had turned down the gas and gone away, and Jack found himself alone in this strange room, away from his mother and Betty, he began to feel very lonely. There was no one to see the tears now, and he let them have their own way at last. He tried to cry very softly, so as not to disturb Winifred in the next room, but in spite of all his efforts the choking sobs would come. Suddenly the door creaked slightly, there was a patter of bare feet on the carpet, and a sweet little voice whispered close at his side:

"Are you asleep, Jack?"

"No," said Jack, speaking in a rather muffled voice, for he had been trying to stifle his sobs by burying his head in the pillow, "I haven't gone to sleep yet, but I guess I shall pretty soon."

"I just came to ask if you would like to have one of the children for company. I know boys don't care much about dolls generally, but they are very comforting sometimes, especially when people don't feel quite happy, and I thought you might possibly like Lord Fauntleroy, because he's a boy too, you know."

"You are very kind," said Jack gratefully; "I should like it. I never do play with dolls—boys don't, you know, but a boy doll—well, that seems a little different, doesn't it?"

"Of course it does," said Winifred confidently. "Just wait a minute, and I'll bring him."

She darted away into her own room, returning in a moment with Lord Fauntleroy in her arms.

"I'll put him right here on the pillow beside you," she said, "and if you should feel lonely, you can just put out your hand and touch him. There isn't anything to be lonely for really, you know, because father and mother are in the parlor, and I'm right here in the next room, but people do sometimes feel a little queer in the dark, especially if they're not used to it. Lulu Bell doesn't like the dark a bit, and she was ten last December. Now I guess we'd better not talk any more, because mother said we were to go right to sleep."

Whether it was the presence of Lord Fauntleroy or the thought of the kind little girl who had brought him I do not know, but, whatever the cause may have been, Jack did not cry any more that night. He lay awake for a little while thinking about how kind every one was, and then his eyes closed, and he fell into a sound sleep from which he did not wake till morning.

CHAPTER VII

A CHANCE FOR JACK

For several days Mrs. Randall was very ill, much worse than Jack ever knew, for no one had the heart to tell him of the anxiety that was filling their minds to the exclusion of almost every other thought. Even Betty had always a bright smile and a cheerful assurance for her little brother that mother would soon be better, no matter how heavy her poor little heart might be. It was impossible to help loving the sweet-tempered, gentle little cripple, and Mr. and Mrs. Hamilton soon found themselves growing very fond of their guest, while Dr. Bell seldom failed to stop for a word or two with his little soldier boy, as he called him, after each of his visits to the invalid upstairs. As for Winifred, she constituted herself Jack's willing slave, and the two soon became firm friends. They read together, played games together, and finally, as a mark of especial favor, Jack undertook to teach her to draw, an honor which was highly appreciated by the little girl.

Lulu Bell, hearing the story from her father, came at once to see the interesting addition to the Hamilton household, and the three children spent a delightful afternoon together, the little girls teaching Jack several new games, and being taught several themselves in return. Betty, coming in for a few moments to see how her brother was getting on, found them all laughing heartily over "My Grandmother's Cat." Jack's eyes were fairly dancing, and there was a brighter tinge of color in his cheeks than she had seen there in many a day. Poor Betty's heart was very heavy that day, and, somehow, the sight of Jack's happiness—a happiness in which she had no share—caused her to feel almost angry, although she could not have told why. It was the first time in his life that Jack had ever enjoyed anything in which his sister had not an equal share.

Winifred greeted Betty very kindly, and Jack begged her to stay and join in the fun, but the little girl only shook her head sadly, saying she must go back to her mother, as Miss Clark might need her.

"But you'll come back very soon, won't you, Betty?" Jack said a little wistfully, lifting his face for a kiss. "Oh, Betty dear, I am having such a good time; I wish you could stay."

Betty found them all laughing heartily over "My Grandmother's Cat."

"I can't," said Betty shortly, and having kissed her little brother she hurried away, winking hard to keep back the tears.

On the stairs she encountered Miss Clark, dressed for her daily walk.

"Your mother is asleep," the nurse explained, "and Mrs. Hamilton is going to sit with her till I come back. Don't look so worried, dear, she isn't any worse to-day; indeed, we think she is a little better."

Betty tried to smile, but the effort was rather a failure, and when she had reached their own apartment, sat down on Jack's sofa, laying her head down on the cushion on which her little brother's head had so often rested.

A few moments later, Mrs. Hamilton, going into the kitchen for something she wanted, was startled by the sound of low, subdued crying. Glancing in at the door of the sitting room she saw Betty lying face downwards on the sofa, her whole frame shaking with sobs. Next instant she was bending over the little figure, softly stroking Betty's tumbled hair.

"Betty," she said tenderly, "poor little Betty, what is it?"

With a start Betty lifted her face, and somewhat to Mrs. Hamilton's surprise, grew suddenly very red.

"It isn't anything," she said, beginning a hasty search for her handkerchief, "only—only, I'm a horrid, wicked girl."

"Betty, dear, what do you mean?" Mrs. Hamilton sat down on the sofa and put an arm affectionately around the trembling child. "Don't you know what a great help you have been to Miss Clark and me? Why, I have never seen a more thoughtful, sensible little girl."

"I am wicked, though," Betty maintained stoutly; "I'm jealous. I don't like to have Jack so happy without me."

Mrs. Hamilton with some difficulty repressed a smile.

"Jealousy is a very common fault in all of us, Betty," she said, "but I am sure you wouldn't like it if Jack were unhappy and fretting."

"No, oh, no, I shouldn't like that!—but"—with a stifled sob—"he did seem to be having such a good time, and I'm so unhappy and so worried about mother."

"I know you are worried about your mother, dear, but we all think her a little better to-day, and Dr. Bell says that if she continues to improve for the next twenty-four hours he hopes she will be out of all danger. And now, Betty, I am going to tell you something that I know you will be glad to hear. It is about Jack."

"About Jack?" repeated Betty, beginning to look interested.

"Yes, dear. I know how dearly you love your little brother, and how happy it would make you if anything could be done for him—anything to help his illness, I mean."

"Oh, Mrs. Hamilton, could anything really——" Betty could say no more, but her flushed cheeks and sparkling eyes were more expressive than words.

"Dr. Bell was talking to me about Jack last evening," Mrs. Hamilton went on. "He is very much interested in the case, and as soon as your mother is well enough he is going to ask her consent to bring a famous surgeon here to see Jack."

Betty was actually trembling with excitement.

"And he thinks—he thinks that something might be done, so that Jack would be able to walk like other people?" she gasped.

"He thinks something might be tried."

"I remember I once heard mother say that when Jack was a baby a doctor told father that if he ever grew strong enough to bear it an operation might be performed. Jack was so delicate for a long time that mother never dared to think of it, but he is much stronger now."

"Well," said Mrs. Hamilton, rising, "we won't talk to any one about it just yet, least of all to Jack himself, because, you know, it might amount to nothing, and then think how terribly disappointed he would be. But you and I can talk about it sometimes, and it will be our little secret."

"Yes," said Betty eagerly, "and as soon as mother is well enough she shall know too. Oh, Mrs. Hamilton, you have made me so very, very happy I don't know what to do."

There was no more jealousy for Betty that day. She went about with a look of such radiant happiness on her face that, when she came to kiss Jack good-night, his first words were an eager exclamation. "Oh, Betty, mother's better; I know she is, or you wouldn't look like that!"

The next morning Mrs. Randall really was better, and Dr. Bell came in after his early visit to tell Jack the good news.

"You have been a good, brave little soldier," he said kindly, "and in a few more days you will be able to go back to your mother and Betty."

"Betty has been much braver, though," said Jack, always eager to sound his sister's praises. "Mrs. Hamilton says she doesn't know what they would have done without Betty."

"Yes, indeed, Betty has been a famous little helper. I shall tell your mother she has two little people to be proud of."

It was still some days, however, before Jack could go home, or before Mrs. Randall was able fully to understand the state of affairs. At first she was too weak to care much about what went on around her. She would lie with half-closed eyes, only smiling faintly when spoken to, and silently accepting all that was done for her without appearing to think very much about it. But as her strength began to return, cares and anxieties returned too, and one morning, when Mrs. Hamilton went up to relieve Miss Clark for an hour, she found the invalid looking so flushed and distressed that she hastened to inquire, as she took the hand Mrs. Randall held out to her, "Is anything wrong? Are you not feeling as well this morning?"

"Oh, yes, I am gaining strength every day," said Mrs. Randall with a sigh, "but, Mrs. Hamilton, how can I ever repay you for all you have done for us? I have been questioning Betty, and she has told me everything."

"Now, my dear Mrs. Randall, please don't let us talk about repaying anything," said Mrs. Hamilton cheerfully. "You haven't the least idea of the pleasure your dear little boy has given my Winifred, and as for any little things that I may have been able to do, why, they have given me real pleasure too."

"You are very good, very good indeed," Mrs. Randall murmured, "but I can't help worrying a little when I think of all that this illness of mine involves. There are so many expenses to think of; the doctor and the nurse, and other things besides. Miss Clark tells me that it will be several weeks yet before I am able to go back to my work, and it is so near the end of the season."

"I told Betty to write to your pupils, telling them of your illness," said Mrs. Hamilton. "We found a list of addresses in your desk. Several notes have come for you, but I was afraid you were not strong enough to see them before. Would you like to read some of them now?"

Mrs. Randall said she would, and when she had opened and glanced over the half-dozen notes Mrs. Hamilton brought her, she looked up with tears in her eyes.

"People are very good," she said a little unsteadily. "I don't think I ever realized it before, but I have a great deal for which to be thankful."

"I don't think we ever do realize what true friendship means until trouble comes," said Mrs. Hamilton gently. "I know I did not until a great sorrow came to me. I now feel that there is no greater happiness in the world than being able to show my friends how much I care for them."

The two ladies had a long talk that morning, and grew to know and like each other better than either would have believed possible before. When Mrs. Hamilton had gone back to her own apartment Mrs. Randall called Betty to her side.

"Betty, darling," she said, and though there were tears in her eyes, there was a more peaceful expression on her face than the little girl had ever seen there before. "I am afraid I have been a very foolish, selfish mother to you and Jack, but we all make mistakes sometimes, and I am going to try and undo mine as soon as I can. Everybody has been so good it makes me ashamed of my old foolish pride. Mrs. Hamilton has taught me a lesson this morning that I shall never forget. I think she is the best woman I have ever known."

That same afternoon Jack came home. Dr. Bell carried him upstairs and laid him on the bed beside his mother. How delightful it was to the little cripple to nestle in his mother's arms once more, and to feel her tender kisses on his face. Neither of them said very much; but their happy faces told the story plainly enough, and the doctor's kind eyes glistened as he turned away rather hurriedly to give some direction to Miss Clark. But after the first few rapturous moments, Jack found his tongue and chattered away, telling of all the pleasant times he had had, and the kind friends he had made, while Mrs. Randall listened; and Betty hovered over them both with such a radiant face that her mother asked her smilingly if she had not something delightful to tell as well as Jack. But Betty only blushed a little and shook her head. She had no intention of disclosing her secret just yet.

"Oh, Betty, it is nice to be at home again," said Jack, stretching himself comfortably on the familiar sofa, when Miss Clark had carried him away to the sitting room, leaving Mrs. Randall to rest for a while. "I've had a perfectly lovely time, but I do like home."

"You don't love Winifred better than me, do you?" said Betty, with a little twinge of the old jealousy.

"Why, Betty, how could I possibly do such a thing as that?" Jack's eyes opened wide in astonishment.

"I didn't know," said Betty, hanging her head. "I'm awfully glad you don't."

"I love Winifred very much," said Jack slowly, "but then you're my own sister, and of course a person couldn't love another person as much as his own sister. Oh, Betty, you didn't really think I could, did you?"

Jack was beginning to look troubled, and Betty, very much ashamed of herself, hastened to reassure him.

"No, no, of course I didn't, not really, you know," she said, giving her brother a hearty kiss. "I was silly, that's all, but it's all right now. Isn't it lovely having mother so much better? Miss Clark says she can begin to sit up in a few days, and such nice things have happened. Nearly all mother's pupils have written kind notes, and most of them have sent checks paying up to the end of the term. I don't think mother wanted to take the checks at first, but Mrs. Hamilton talked to her, and she says she's going to try not to mind so much about accepting favors any more. I think there is only just one other thing in the world that could make me happier than I am to-day."

"What's that?" Jack inquired.

"To have you able to walk," said Betty softly. She turned her head away as she spoke, so that her brother should not see the expression in her eyes.

Jack gave a little start, and drew a long, deep breath.

"But, Betty," he said almost in a whisper, "that's something that couldn't ever possibly happen, you know. Oh, Betty, dear, please don't talk about it, because you see it's impossible."

Suddenly Betty laid her face down beside her brother's on the pillow, with a sob.

"Very, very wonderful things do happen sometimes," she whispered, "things that are almost as wonderful as fairy stories. If you ever could be made to walk, Jack, wouldn't you be the very happiest boy in the whole world?"

"Of course I should," said Jack with decision, "if it only could happen, but then you know, it couldn't."

Betty said no more, but hugged Jack tight, and kissed him a great many times, and then she went away to the kitchen to help Miss Clark get dinner.

CHAPTER VIII

THE DOCTOR'S VERDICT

Miss Clark's prediction proved correct, and in a few days Mrs. Randall was able to sit up, and to be helped into the sunny little parlor, where she sat by Jack's sofa, looking happier and more at rest than the children had ever seen her look before. After that she improved so rapidly that even Dr. Bell was surprised, and declared he had never seen a woman with a finer constitution. At the end of another week Miss Clark went away to another case, and Mrs. Flynn, the good-natured Irishwoman who did the Randalls' washing, was engaged to come in by the day. So the bright spring days came and went, and when the sun was brightest and the air warmest, Jack's pale face would often look a little wistful, but nothing more was said about drives in the park, and Betty, still waiting patiently for leave to reveal her secret, began to wonder if after all Mrs. Hamilton had been mistaken, or Dr. Bell had changed his mind.

One Saturday morning in May, Winifred appeared shortly after breakfast, looking pleased and excited, and bringing an invitation for Betty.

"It's from Lulu Bell," she explained, when Betty, quite thrilled at the prospect, had brought the visitor into the parlor to tell the news to her mother and Jack. "Lulu asked Gertie Rossiter and me to lunch with her and go to the circus to-day, but Gertie has the measles, so Lulu telephoned, and asked me to bring Betty instead. Mother says she hopes you'll let Betty go, Mrs. Randall, because she's sure Mrs. Bell would like to have her very much."

Mrs. Randall looked pleased.

"I am sure Betty would enjoy it," she said; "you would like to go, wouldn't you, dear?"

Betty hesitated, and glanced a little uneasily at Jack.

"I should like it," she said. "I've never been to the circus and it must be lovely, but—but——"

"Oh, Betty, you must go!" cried Jack eagerly. "It'll be so nice, and you can tell me all about it when you come home."

The time had been, and not so long before either, when Mrs. Randall would have been inclined to regard this invitation as an attempt at patronage, but she had been learning more than one lesson in these days of her convalescence, and Mrs. Hamilton's kindly advice was beginning to bear fruit.

"Lulu says her mother doesn't want us to wear anything especially nice," Winifred went on, "because we shall go around to see the animals before the circus begins, and it may be dusty. I've got a lovely new book out of the library; it's called 'Dorothy Dainty,' and I'm going to bring it up for Jack to read this afternoon. I know he'll like it."

Matters being thus happily arranged, Winifred hurried away to telephone her friend that Betty would be delighted to accept the invitation, and Betty made herself very useful, helping Mrs. Flynn with the Saturday cleaning, feeling all the time as if she were about to enter upon a new and very interesting experience.

"You're sure you don't mind, Jack," she said, stooping to kiss him at the last moment before going downstairs to join Winifred.

"Not a bit," said Jack heartily. "I hope you'll have a lovely time, and it'll be such fun to hear all about it."

"You're not a single mite jealous, are you?" said Betty, with a sudden recollection of her own feelings on another occasion.

"No, of course not. What does it feel like to be jealous?"

"Well, you know, I never went away and left you for a whole afternoon, just to have fun before, and I'm going to have a good time, and you're not. You wouldn't like it if you were jealous."

"But I am going to have a nice time," said Jack, looking rather puzzled; "I've got that nice book Winifred brought, and mother's going to play for me. I wonder what being jealous really does feel like."

"It doesn't feel nice," said Betty, blushing, "but I don't believe you'll ever know anything about it, you're too dear."

It was about twelve o'clock when the two little girls, accompanied by Mrs. Hamilton, left the apartment house, and started on their walk across the park, to the Bells' home on Madison Avenue. It was a beautiful day, and the park was full of children, all making the most of their Saturday holiday. They met several May parties, and Betty told them how her mother had once read them Tennyson's "May Queen," and how Jack had been so much interested in the poem that he had learned it by heart.

"Jack is really a very clever boy," said Winifred admiringly. "I don't like boys very much generally, they're so rough, but I respect Jack very much indeed."

"There isn't any other boy in the world like him," said Betty, with conviction. "Mrs. Hamilton," she added rather shyly, "do you suppose Dr. Bell has forgotten Jack, now that he doesn't come to see mother any more?"

"I am very sure he has not," said Mrs. Hamilton decidedly.

Betty said no more on the subject, but her heart beat high with renewed hope, and during the rest of the walk she felt as if she were treading upon air.

Betty could not help feeling a little uncomfortable when she first caught sight of the handsome house where Winifred's friends lived. She had met Lulu only once, and although she looked upon the doctor as one of her best friends, she did not know any other members of the family, and the thought of being presented to entire strangers was a rather embarrassing one. Mrs. Hamilton, having another engagement, left them at the foot of the steps. Winifred rang the bell, and when the door was opened by the boy in brass buttons, she walked in with the air of a person very much at home. Betty followed more slowly, wondering rather uncomfortably what people who lived in such a grand-looking house would think of her faded brown dress and last year's straw hat. But all such speculations were speedily forgotten in the kind cordiality of the greeting she received. Lulu was a charming little hostess, and her mother and her blind aunt both greeted the little stranger so kindly, that they soon succeeded in making her feel almost as much at home as Winifred herself.

At luncheon the ladies asked questions about Jack, and quite won Betty's heart by telling her of the many kind things the doctor had said about her little brother. Lulu had a great deal to say about the pretty seaside cottage her father had just hired for the summer.

"You must come and make us a long visit, Winifred," she said decidedly, but Winifred shook her head.

"I can't leave mother," she said, with equal decision on her part. "It's so perfectly beautiful to have her, I can't ever go away from her."

"There is a good hotel very near us," said Mrs. Bell kindly. "Perhaps your father and mother will come there to board for a while."

But Winifred still looked doubtful. She had an idea that money was not very plentiful with her family just then, and she had heard her mother say that a couple of weeks in the mountains, while father had his vacation, would probably be all they could afford that summer.

What a delightful afternoon that was!

As soon as they rose from the luncheon table Mrs. Bell and the three little girls started for the circus.

What a delightful afternoon that was! Even Betty's wildest anticipations had scarcely prepared her for the blissful reality. She enjoyed every moment, and every incident, from the clown who made her laugh till she cried, to the "Battle of Santiago," which made her shiver and cling tightly to Winifred's hand.

"It's been the loveliest afternoon I ever knew," she said gratefully to Mrs. Bell, when it was all over, and the little girls were saying good-bye at the door of the apartment house. "It was so kind of you to take me, and I shall have lots and lots to tell Jack."

"I am very glad you could come with us, dear," said Mrs. Bell, smiling kindly, "and next year I hope we can take Jack with us too."

"I suppose it isn't a very nice thing to say," Lulu whispered to Winifred, "but I can't help being a little glad Gertie has the measles. I do like Betty ever so much, and I know mamma likes her too."

At the door of the Hamiltons' apartment the children separated, and Betty ran gayly upstairs, thinking of the delightful time she should have living the events of the afternoon all over again in describing them to Jack. She opened the front door with her key, and was just going to call out to her mother and Jack, when something in the unusual stillness of the place caused her to pause suddenly.

"Perhaps mother's lying down," she said to herself, "and Jack doesn't like to make any noise for fear of disturbing her. I'll go in softly and see."

She stole on tiptoe to the sitting room door, and peeped in. Her mother was not there, but Jack was lying on the sofa as usual. At sight of her the little fellow started up and held out his arms. One glance at his face was enough to convince Betty that something had happened.

"What is it, Jack?" she whispered, running to his side, and beginning to tremble with a strange new sensation, but whether of joy or fear she did not know. "What makes you look so—so queer? Where's mother?"

"Mother's in her room," said Jack; "she shut the door; she's gone to lie down, I guess." His voice trembled, and he hid his face on Betty's shoulder.

"But something has happened, I know it has," persisted Betty, trembling more than ever. "Oh, Jack, what is it?"

"Betty," said Jack softly, "do you remember what you said the other day, about—about the thing that would make you happier than anything else, even than mother's getting well?"

"You mean the thing about you—oh, Jack, you mean about your being made to walk?"

Jack nodded.

"Tell me quick," gasped Betty breathlessly, the circus and everything else forgotten in the excitement of this wonderful news.

"Well, Doctor Bell came this afternoon right after lunch, and there was another doctor with him. He was rather old, and not so nice as Dr. Bell, but I think he wanted to be very kind. First they went in the dining room, and talked to mother for a little while, and I think I heard mother crying. Then they came in here, and looked at me. What they did hurt a good deal, but I tried not to mind, because Dr. Bell called me a brave soldier boy. Then they went back to the dining room, and talked some more to mother, and the new doctor went away. After that mother and Dr. Bell came back here. Mother was crying a good deal, but she looked awfully glad too, and they told me what it all meant. Next week I'm to go to a hospital, and have an operation. It won't hurt, Dr. Bell says, because they'll give me something to make me go to sleep, and when I get better, they think—they're not quite sure—but they really do think, that I shall be able to walk."

CHAPTER IX

SUSPENSE

It was very quiet in the Randalls' apartment one warm spring afternoon. For nearly two hours the only sounds to break the utter stillness had been the ticking of the clock and an occasional movement from the kitchen, where Mrs. Flynn tiptoed softly about, preparing dinner. Mrs. Randall sat in the armchair by the open window. Her face was white and set, and sometimes her lips moved, but no sound came from them. Betty felt sure that her mother was saying her prayers. It seemed to Betty as though a month must have passed since the morning. She had tried to read, to sew, to do anything to pass the terrible hours of suspense, but it was of no use, and now she sat on a stool at her mother's feet resting her head against Mrs. Randall's knee. She was trying very hard to be brave, but she knew that if she dared glance even for a moment at Jack's empty sofa, she would no longer be able to choke down the rising sobs, or keep back the tears which seemed so near the surface.

Early that morning Jack had been taken away to the hospital, and even as they sat there in silence, Betty and her mother knew the work was being done which was to decide the fate of the little boy for life.

The doctors had decided that it would be best to perform the operation before hot weather set in, and besides, as Dr. Bell wisely explained to Mrs. Randall, it would never do to keep the child in suspense any longer than necessary, now that he knew what was impending. Mrs. Randall was not yet strong enough to leave the house, but Dr. Bell had come himself for Jack, and Mrs. Hamilton had gone with them to the hospital, promising to remain until the operation was over. Jack had been very brave and cheerful, and the excitement had helped every one up to the last moment. Dr. Bell had told funny stories to make them all laugh, and Mrs. Hamilton had talked about the nice things they would bring Jack when they came to the hospital to see him. No one had cried, only, just as the last good-byes were being said, Jack had suddenly thrown his arms round his mother's neck and clung to her, and Mrs. Randall had clasped him close to her heart, and held him there in a silence that was far more expressive than any words. And now it was afternoon, and Betty and her mother were waiting, in silent, breathless suspense, for the news that they both knew must come before long. Mrs. Hamilton had promised to let them know the moment the operation was over.

The door creaked softly and Mrs. Flynn came in with a cup of tea in her hand.

"Take a drop of tea, dearie, do," she whispered soothingly, bending over Mrs. Randall's chair; "it'll put heart into ye."

Mrs. Randall shook her head impatiently.

"Not now, Mrs. Flynn; I couldn't touch anything now, it would choke me. Perhaps by and by——"

Mrs. Flynn turned away with a sigh, and went back to the kitchen, beckoning to Betty to follow her.

"Can't you do nothin' to cheer her up a bit, darlin'," she whispered, when Betty joined her in the kitchen. "Not a mouthful of anything has she touched this whole blessed day, and it's awful to see her sittin' lookin' like that, her that's just off a sick bed too."

"She's thinking about Jack," said Betty sadly; "she can't eat till she knows; I couldn't eat either, Mrs. Flynn."

Mrs. Flynn sighed again, and set down the teacup.

"Well, you'll hear pretty soon now, I guess," she said, with an air of resignation, "and I've got some nice strong chicken soup on the stove. A cup of that'll do yez both good by and by."

"Oh, Mrs. Flynn," whispered Betty, drawing close to the kind-hearted Irish-woman, "I'm so frightened. I don't know why, but I am. You don't think, do you, that anything dreadful is going to happen?"

"Not a bit of it, darlin'," said Mrs. Flynn reassuringly. "Jack'll be all right, the little angel, and we'll have him back, and runnin' about like any one else in just no time at all. Why, I shouldn't wonder if we'd see him ridin' one of them bicycles on Fifth Avenue next month."

"But people don't always get over operations, you know, Mrs. Flynn," said Betty, with a choke in her voice.

"Nonsense," retorted Mrs. Flynn, with an indignant toss of her head. "Sure, didn't me brother-in-law's first cousin have the two legs of him took off wid a trolley-car on Lexington Avenue, and ain't he walkin' around now 'most as good as ever on two cork stumps, as they give him at the hospital? There ain't nothin' them doctors can't do, barrin' raisin' the dead."

A ring at the door bell at this moment put an end to the Irish-woman's hopeful predictions. Betty uttered a little half-frightened cry, and Mrs. Flynn flew to open the door. Mrs. Randall sprang from her chair, and was in the hall before Mrs. Flynn had left the kitchen. Next moment, however, there was a little sigh of disappointment from every one; the visitor was only Winifred.

"I thought I'd come to see you for a little while," she explained to Betty, who was trying to smile, and not show the disappointment she felt. "It's lonely downstairs without mother, and I've done all my lessons. I've brought Miss Mollie; I thought you might like to have her."

"I am very glad to have her," said Betty, taking the doll in her arms. She was not very fond of dolls, but she wanted to show Winifred that she appreciated her kindness. "Let's go into my room, where we can talk and not disturb mother."

They were moving away, but Mrs. Randall called them back.

"Stay here, children," she said, and her voice sounded sharp from anxiety. "I like to hear you talk, and you don't disturb me."

So the two little girls went into the parlor, and sat down side by side on Jack's sofa, Betty still holding Miss Mollie in her arms. They were both very silent at first, and Winifred kept casting sympathetic glances towards Mrs. Randall, who had now left her seat, and was standing with her back to them, looking out of the window. But after a little while they began to talk in whispers.

"I guess mother will be back pretty soon now," said Winifred, giving Betty's cold little hand an encouraging squeeze. "She'll be sure to come and tell you about Jack the very first thing."

Betty said nothing, and after a little pause Winifred went on.

"Won't it be lovely when Jack gets well? Just think, he may be a soldier after all when he grows up. You know Dr. Bell always calls him a little soldier boy."

"He'd like to be one," said Betty, brightening at the thought; "our grandfather was a general, you know."

"Yes, and even if he never goes to war, I think he is much braver now than a great many real soldiers are. Father says there are not many little boys only nine years old who would be willing to go away and stay all by themselves in a big, strange hospital."

"Don't let's talk about that," said Betty, beginning to cry. "I can't bear to think of his being all by himself."

"Oh, but he won't be, not really. Lulu has been to that hospital to see the children and take them things, and she says the nurses are very kind. One of them took care of Lulu's aunt when she broke her knee last year, and they all liked her very much. And then, you know, Dr. Bell goes there every day, and we shall go too, just as soon as Jack is well enough to see us. Oh, Betty, dear, I'm sure God is going to let Jack get well and be just like other people. I've been saying little prayers to Him all day about it."

"So have I," said Betty, who was beginning to find Winifred's society very cheering. "He'll be so happy if he can walk, and mother says Dr. Bell wants us all to go to the country as soon as Jack is strong enough."

Winifred heaved a little sigh.

"I think almost every one is going to the country pretty soon," she said. "School closes the end of next week, and all the girls are going away the first part of June. I shall miss them all, especially Lulu."

"Dr. Bell said they were going to the seashore the first of June."

"Yes, they're going to Navesink; Lulu says it's a lovely place. There's the ocean, you know, and a river, where they can fish and catch crabs. I've never seen the ocean; Aunt Estelle doesn't like sea air, so we always went to the mountains."

"Wouldn't you like to go to Navesink too?" Betty asked.

"I should just love it. Lulu wants me to come and visit her, but of course I can't leave mother."

"New York isn't so bad in summer," said Betty cheerfully. "We were here last year. It's nice in the park and on the Riverside, but of course the real country must be much nicer."

"I think any place is nice where mother is," said Winifred, with simple conviction. "Oh, Betty, there's the door bell, and it's mother's ring."

Betty sprang to her feet, and darted out into the hall. Mrs. Randall took a few quick steps towards the door, but then her strength failed her, and, with a low cry, she sank on her knees on the floor beside Jack's sofa, trembling from head to foot, and covering her face with her hands.

Mrs. Hamilton came straight into the room. She passed the two little girls without a word, but there was a look on her sweet face that somehow kept them both silent, eager as they were for news. For one second she paused beside the sofa, and then dropping on her own knees, took the trembling, swaying figure right into her kind arms.

"Oh, my dear, my dear," she sobbed, the happy tears streaming down her cheeks, "I don't know how to tell you, but it is all as we wished. The operation is over; it was a great success, the doctors say, and—and—don't tremble so, dear—there is nothing to grieve over, but, oh, so much to make you glad. I have just come from the hospital, and Dr. Bell has sent you this message. 'Tell Mrs. Randall,' he said, and there were tears in his eyes, 'tell Mrs. Randall that everything is going on splendidly,' and—and—oh, think of it, my dear,—'that her little boy will walk.'"

CHAPTER X

A LETTER AND A SURPRISE

"Here's a letter for you, Winnie," said Mr. Hamilton, coming into the dining room, just as his wife and little daughter were sitting down to breakfast one warm morning in the beginning of July.

"It's from Lulu," exclaimed Winifred joyfully, glancing at the handwriting. "Oh, I'm so glad! I haven't had a letter from her since she went away."

"This is a good fat one, at any rate," said Mr. Hamilton, smiling, and Mrs. Hamilton added:

"Read it to us, dear."

So Winifred opened her letter and began:

"NAVESINK, N.J., July th.

"DEAREST WINIFRED:

"I meant to write to you ever so long ago, but I have been so busy that I couldn't find the time. This is a lovely place, and we all like it very much. The ocean is right in front of the house, and in the big storm last week the waves came up all over the lawn. We go in bathing every day that the ocean is smooth enough, all but Aunt Daisy. She is afraid of the big waves, but papa says she wouldn't be if she would only make up her mind to go in once. On the other side of the house is the Shrewsbury River, and that is very nice too. All the Rossiters came up to spend the day last Saturday, and papa took us crabbing. I caught three, and we had them for luncheon. There is an old boat fastened to our dock. It hasn't any oars, or rudder, or anything, but it's splendid to play shipwreck in.

"I see the Randalls almost every day. The house where they are boarding is only a little way from our cottage. Jack looks ever so much better than when he came, and papa says the sea air is making him stronger every day.

He can stand all by himself now, and walk a little with his crutches. Papa thinks by the autumn he will be able to walk as well as anybody. Mamma has given him a go-cart, and Betty and I push him about in it. We all go down to the beach, and when we have made a nice seat in the sand for Jack, he gets out of the go-cart and sits there. I like Betty and Jack ever so much, and mamma likes to have me play with them.

"Mrs. Randall has a good many pupils already, and mamma thinks she will have more by and by, when all the summer people get here. Aunt Daisy is taking music lessons from her, and says she is the best teacher she ever had. She plays beautifully too. Mamma had her come over and play for some people the other day, and they all enjoyed it very much.

"I am having a lovely time, but I do miss you very much. Can't you really come and make me a visit? Mamma and Aunt Daisy would love to have you, and there are two beds in my room. I should be so very, very happy if you would only come.

"My hand is getting tired, so I shall have to stop.

"Betty and Jack send their love, and say they would love it if you would come. Please answer this letter right away, and believe me, with lots of love and kisses,

> "Your   true   friend,
> "LOUISE M. BELL."

"That's a lovely letter," said Winifred in a tone of profound admiration. "Lulu writes beautifully, don't you think so, mother?"

"She certainly expresses herself very well," said Mrs. Hamilton, smiling.

"She writes stories too," Winifred went on, putting her letter carefully back into the envelope; "she intends to be an authoress when she grows up. She did think once that she would be a missionary, but now she has decided that she would rather be an authoress like her aunt."

"Wouldn't you like to go to Navesink and make Lulu a visit?" Mr. Hamilton asked.

Winifred looked a little wistful, but she shook her head decidedly.

"Not without mother. If mother could go too, I should love it better than anything else in the world."

Mr. and Mrs. Hamilton exchanged glances, but they were both silent, and nothing more was said on the subject.

As soon as they rose from the breakfast table, Winifred went to put her letter away in the little box where she kept all her treasures, but before doing so she sat down on the edge of her bed, and read it all over again from beginning to end. When she had finished, her face looked even more wistful than before.

"I should like to go, oh, I should like it very much," she said, with a long sigh, "but I couldn't go anywhere without mother. I suppose when people have only had mothers a little while like me, they feel differently about leaving them from the people who have had them all the time."

The fact was, Winifred was feeling a little bit lonely. It was very warm in the city, and now that school was over, and all her friends had left town, she found time hang somewhat heavy on her hands. The children were a great comfort, of course, and her mother was everything to her, but she missed the work and the companionship of school, and there were times on those hot summer days when even story books seemed to have lost their charms.

She and Betty had become great friends during the time when Jack was in the hospital, and when Dr. Bell had decided that the seashore was the place for Jack, and the Randalls had given up their flat, and gone for the summer to board at Navesink—the kind doctor having procured accommodation for them in a house not far from his own—Winifred, although rejoicing heartily in her friends' good fortune, could not help feeling very forlorn without them. It was two weeks now since the Randalls had gone away, and Lulu's letter was the first news Winifred had received from any of her friends.

On this particular morning things were unusually dull. It was very hot, for one thing, and then her mother and Lizzie were both very busy in the kitchen, putting up strawberry preserves. Lulu's letter had suggested so many pleasant possibilities too. Certainly sea bathing and playing shipwreck in a real boat sounded much more attractive than reading story books in a hot little bedroom on the second floor of a New York apartment house. She did her duty faithfully by the children; dressed them all; set Lord Fauntleroy, Rose-Florence, and Lily-Bell at their lessons, arranged Miss Mollie's hair in the latest fashion, and gave Violet-May a dose of castor oil. Then when there was really nothing more to be done for her family, and she had learned from her mother that her services were not desired in the kitchen, she took up "Denise and Ned Toodles," and settling herself in the coolest spot she could find, tried to forget other things in the interest of a new story.

"Well, mousie, here you are; deep in a story book as usual."

At the sound of the familiar voice, Winifred dropped her book, and sprang up with an exclamation of pleasure.

"Oh, Aunt Estelle, I am glad to see you!" she cried joyfully, running to greet the tall, bright-faced young lady who was standing in the doorway. "How did you get in? I never heard the bell."

"I didn't ring, the door was open," said her aunt, laughing and kissing her. "I've been here for some time, talking to your mother in the kitchen, and now I've come to have a little talk with you."

"Won't you sit down?" said Winifred, hospitably drawing forward the comfortable rocker in which she had been sitting. "You look awfully warm. You sit here, and I'll fan you; that'll be nice."

"What have you been reading?" Mrs. Meredith asked, as her little niece perched herself on the arm of her chair, and began swaying a large palm-leaf fan back and forth.

"'Denise and Ned Toodles.' It's a very nice story. Mother got it out of the library for me yesterday. It's all about a little girl who lived in the country and had a pony."

"Do you think you would like to live in the country?" her aunt asked, smiling.

"Yes, I think so; I should like it in the summer, at any rate. Oh, Aunt Estelle, I had such a lovely letter from Lulu this morning. Would you like to see it?"

"Yes, very much, but not just now, for I am in a hurry. I am going downtown to do some errands, and then I am coming back here, and, Winnie, I want you to be ready to go home with me to spend the night."

"To spend the night?" Winifred repeated, looking very much surprised.

"Yes; Uncle Will was grumbling this morning, because he says he never sees anything of you nowadays. We are going to the country on Saturday, you know, and this will be our last chance of having you with us for ever so long."

"I'd like to go if mother says so," said Winifred, rather pleased at the prospect of this little change.

"Oh, that's all right; everything is arranged, and here comes your mother to speak for herself."

Winifred turned eagerly to Mrs. Hamilton, who had just entered the room.

"Mother, Aunt Estelle wants me to go home with her to spend the night. May I go?"

"Yes, dear," said her mother, smiling, "I should like to have you go. I expect to be very busy this afternoon, and Aunt Estelle says Uncle Will wants to see you very much."

"Norah is cleaning silver to-day," Mrs. Meredith said, as she rose to go. "You should have seen her face when I told her I was coming for you."

Winifred looked flattered.

"I always helped Norah clean silver," she said, "and sometimes I used to read to her. I'll take 'Denise and Ned Toodles' and read this afternoon."

The matter having been thus arranged, Mrs. Meredith hurried away to do her errands, promising to return for Winifred in a couple of hours.

"You're sure you won't miss me very much, mother," Winifred said anxiously, as she was bidding her mother good-bye. "It's only for one night, you know, and that is quite different from going away for a real visit."

"Of course it is," said Mrs. Hamilton, laughing. "Now run along with Aunt Estelle, sweetheart, and have a good time. I will come for you early to-morrow morning."

"Mother does seem very busy to-day," remarked Winifred, rather wonderingly, as she walked along by her aunt's side. "I wonder what she's going to do this afternoon. It can't be the preserves, because they're 'most done."

Mrs. Meredith made no answer, and Winifred soon forgot her curiosity in the interest of other subjects. But she would have wondered a good deal more if she could have heard the words her mother was at that moment saying to Lizzie, for no sooner had the door closed behind Winifred and her aunt than Mrs. Hamilton hurried back to the kitchen.

"We can begin right away now, Lizzie," she said, laughing; "the darling is safely out of the way for the rest of the day, and we shall have to work like beavers to accomplish all we have to do. In the first place, I want you to come with me to the storeroom, and help me to get out that big trunk."

Winifred had a very pleasant afternoon. She helped Norah with the silver, and read aloud to her, and then there were Hannah, the German cook, and Josephine, the French maid, to be talked to, and they both seemed much pleased to see her. In the evening Uncle Will and Aunt Estelle made much of her, and when bedtime came, although she missed her mother's good-night kiss, still it seemed so natural to be going to bed in the old familiar nursery, where she had spent so many nights, that she could almost fancy the past happy months were all a dream, and that her mother had never come back from California at all.

"Only no dream could possibly be so lovely as it really is," she said to herself, settling herself comfortably on her pillow when Aunt Estelle had put out the light and gone away. "Oh, I am glad it isn't a dream, but something really true. I was a wicked girl to wish I could go to the country and do something different, when I've got such lots and lots of things to be happy about."

"This is the very perfection of a summer's day," Mr. Meredith remarked at the breakfast table next morning. "I wish I were not obliged to spend it cooped up in my office. A trip to the seaside now would be very much to my liking."

"We're going to take excursions sometimes this summer," said Winifred brightly. "Father says perhaps we may go down to Manhattan Beach for a Sunday. Did you ever go to Manhattan Beach, Uncle Will?"

"Yes, several times. I have been to Navesink too. Isn't that where your friends, the Bells, are spending the summer?"

"Yes; Lulu says it's a beautiful place. She asked me to come for a visit, but I can't leave mother."

"Too bad, isn't it?" observed Mr. Meredith, with his eyes on his plate. "Halloo, there's the door bell; I wonder who can be coming to see us so early in the morning."

"Why, it's father and mother," exclaimed Winifred joyfully, springing down from her chair, and darting out into the hall as Norah opened the front door. "Oh, mother, dear, you are early. We've only just finished breakfast."

"It is such a lovely morning," said Mrs. Hamilton, returning her little daughter's rapturous embrace, "that your father and I thought we would take a trip down the bay."

"Oh, how nice," cried Winifred, clapping her hands. "And isn't it funny? Uncle Will and I have just been talking about trips. Are you sure you can really get away for a whole day, father?"

"I think I can manage it," said Mr. Hamilton, laughing. "Now run and get ready, little one, for our boat leaves at ten, and it's after nine already."

Winifred flew upstairs for her belongings, told the good news to Josephine, and was back again in less than five minutes. She found her father and mother in the dining room with Uncle Will and Aunt Estelle. They had evidently been talking about something which amused them, for every one was smiling, but as soon as Winifred came in Mr. and Mrs. Hamilton rose to go.

"Good-bye, Winnie darling," said Mrs. Meredith, kissing her little niece affectionately, "it has been like a bit of old times having you back with us. You won't forget to write, Mollie?" she added in a lower tone to Mrs. Hamilton, as the two ladies went out into the hall together.

"Good-bye, mousie, and don't forget us," said Uncle Will, as Winifred lifted her face for his good-bye kiss. "I don't know how we shall manage to get on without you all summer."

"Why, mother," said Winifred, looking puzzled, as they hurried away towards the elevated railroad station, "Uncle Will and Aunt Estelle said good-bye just as if they weren't going to see us again, and they're not going to the country till Saturday."

"Perhaps they were afraid something might prevent our meeting again before they leave," said Mrs. Hamilton, rather evasively.

That sail down the bay was a new and very delightful experience to Winifred. She had never traveled much, and every new object of interest was a delight to her. The big, crowded steamboat, the beautiful bay, the Statue of Liberty, and the other interesting sights made the little girl feel as if she could not take in so many new wonders all at once, and she asked innumerable questions about everything, all of which her father and mother answered readily.

That sail down the bay was a new and delightful experience.

"What are we going to do when we get to the place where the boat stops?" she inquired anxiously, as they passed the Floating Hospital. "Must we go right back to New York again?"

"Well, I think we will go a little way in a train first," said Mr. Hamilton, trying to look grave, although his eyes twinkled. "It would be rather a pity to go so far without seeing the ocean, don't you think so?"

"Oh, are we really going to see the ocean?" cried Winifred joyfully. "I think this is one of the nicest things that ever happened."

At the Atlantic Highlands they left the boat, and got into a train, which they found waiting at the pier. There were several trains, in fact, and a great many people seemed to be getting into them. Winifred wondered where they were all going, and if any of the other children she saw were having half as good a time as she was.

"Look, Winnie, there is the ocean," her mother said eagerly, as the train rushed across a long bridge, and a whiff of sea air blew in their faces.

"Where, where?" gasped Winifred, stretching her neck out of the car window. "Oh, I see. Why, how big it is. I never saw water like that before. Do you suppose it looks like this at Navesink?"

"I should not be at all surprised if it looked very much like it," said Mrs. Hamilton, laughing.

At that moment the train began to slacken speed.

"Navesink, Navesink," shouted the brakeman, putting his head in at the car door.

"Isn't it the very loveliest surprise you ever had?" demanded Lulu Bell, dancing up and down on the platform, and hugging Winifred tight. "I never knew a single thing about it till last night, but mamma has known for ever so long, and papa engaged the rooms at the hotel for you. Why, Winifred, don't look as if you were just waking up. It's the nicest thing in the world. You're all going to stay at the hotel for a month, and your father's going to town every day the same as papa does. They wanted it to be a surprise for you. See, here's Betty, and Jack's right over there in the go-cart. We all came down to the station to meet you, and it seemed as if the train would never come, we were so excited."

"Oh," gasped Winifred, finding her voice at last, "it's the very most beautiful thing that could possibly have happened. Are you quite sure it's all true, and not a dream?"

CHAPTER XI

AT NAVESINK

"I think the sea is the most beautiful thing in the world," said Jack, laying down his drawing pencil, and settling himself comfortably in the warm sand. "I could just sit and look at it all day long."

"Is your sketch finished?" inquired Winifred, looking up from the sand fort she was building.

"Yes, do you want to see it?" And Jack held out a sheet of foolscap for his friend's inspection. Jack was a very different-looking boy from the pale little cripple of two months before. There was a light in his eyes and a color in his cheeks that no one had ever seen there since the day of his babyhood. The healthy outdoor life in the bracing sea air was doing wonders for him. Winifred examined the sketch admiringly.

"It's perfectly lovely," she announced. "That fishing boat with the man in it looks as natural as can be. I think you will be a splendid artist when you grow up, Jack."

Jack flushed with pleasure at this frank praise.

"I hope I shall," he said, "I want to be. You know my father was an artist."

"You will be an artist and Lulu will be an authoress," said Winifred reflectively. "I wish Betty and I could both be something nice too."

"I'm afraid I shall never be anything in particular, unless it's a housekeeper," remarked Betty from her seat on the bathing house steps. "I like to sweep and dust and cook better than anything else."

"You'll be a greater sewer, I think," said Winifred, with an admiring glance at the stocking her friend was darning. "Mother says she never saw a little girl who could sew as well as you can."

"Perhaps I shall be a trained nurse. I think I should like being a comfort to sick people. I heard Lulu's aunt say the nurse she had when she broke her knee was a great comfort to her."

"Miss Clark was a great comfort to us when mother was ill," said Betty; "mother had a letter from her yesterday. What's the matter, Jack—are mosquitoes biting?"

"No," said Jack, frowning, "it isn't the mosquitoes, it's only I don't like to have you talk about being things when you grow up."

"Why not?" inquired Betty in astonishment.

"Because if I'm an artist I can take care of you and mother. I want you just to be ladies."

"Well, mother's a lady, isn't she? and she works; and Lulu's aunt writes books."

Jack looked puzzled.

"I don't know quite how to say it," he said slowly, "but I want you to be the kind of ladies that mother was when she lived in England; the kind that live in castles, and have parks and things. They never work, do they?"

Both little girls laughed, and Betty said practically:

"I guess even queens work sometimes, but I know what you mean, Jack, only I think I'd like to be a housekeeper better."

"Here comes Lulu," exclaimed Winifred, rising to meet her friend, who came hurrying along the sand from the direction of her own home. "I've brought some ginger-snaps," announced Lulu, when she had greeted the others, and seated herself beside Betty on the bathing house steps. "I thought we might be hungry before luncheon time. I could have come before, but I was very busy writing my story. Is yours done yet, Winifred?"

"No," said Winifred, blushing; "I don't think I can write stories very well. When I get the ink and paper, and everything ready, I never can think of anything to say."

"Oh, but you must go on trying," urged Lulu. "It's the easiest thing in the world when you once get started. Does Betty know about what we're doing?"

"No," said Betty, looking interested, "tell me about it."

"Why, you see," Lulu explained, "Aunt Daisy is writing a book, and in it two little girls have to write compositions, and she thought it would be so nice to have original ones written by real little girls. So she asked Winifred and me to write some for her, and if she likes them well enough, she will put them in her book, and they will be published. Won't that be fun?"

Betty and Jack were both much impressed, and Winifred, who did not find authorship come at all easy, was struck with a bright idea.

"I don't suppose your aunt cares who writes the stories, so long as she gets them, does she, Lulu?"

"Why, no, I don't suppose so," Lulu admitted, "but you really must try, Winnie. Think how grand it will be to have something published."

"I was only thinking that perhaps Betty or Jack could do it better," said Winifred, with an appealing glance at her two little friends, both of whom, however, declined to enter the compact, declaring that they couldn't write a story to save their lives.

"I can't see why you all find it so hard," said Lulu a little patronizingly; "it seems very easy to me. I was only five when I made up my first story, and Aunt Daisy wrote it down on her typewriter. It wasn't very long, only 'Two little girls went to see two little boys. They played hide and seek and blindman's buff. Then they had ice cream, and went home again.' Aunt Daisy said it was a beginning, and I've been writing stories ever since. Oh, by the way, Aunt Daisy says if you'll come over this afternoon she'll tell us all stories on the piazza."

The children looked pleased, and accepted the invitation with alacrity, for Lulu's blind aunt was a famous story-teller and a great favorite with them all.

"Papa and mamma have gone to the city for the day," said Lulu, "and Aunt Daisy's very busy this morning, writing on her story, but she's promised to devote the whole afternoon to us."

The conversation drifted to other things, and the next hour passed very pleasantly in building sand forts, making mud pies, and doing other delightful things only possible at the sea shore. The ocean was very calm, and the little girls took off their shoes and stockings, and let the little waves splash over their feet. Jack lay on the sand, watching them and making sketches by turns. Some of the people from the hotels and cottages came down to the beach to bathe, and almost every one had a pleasant word for the little boy.

At last the ginger-snaps were produced, and they all sat down to enjoy them before going home.

"I wonder what makes people so dreadfully hungry at the sea shore," remarked Jack, helping himself to his third ginger-snap. "At home I never used to eat very much."

"It's because you're so much better than you used to be," said Betty, regarding her brother with happy, loving eyes. "What's the matter, Lulu? you've dropped your cake."

"My goodness," exclaimed Lulu, clasping her hands in dismay. "I declare I forgot all about telling you the most important thing. A lord is coming to stay with us."

"A what?" inquired Betty and Winifred both together.

"A lord," repeated Lulu impressively, "a real live English lord. He's coming on his yacht. Papa got a letter from him yesterday, and he's on his way now."

"Where is he coming from?" Winifred asked.

"I don't know, but he's traveling in his yacht. He has a castle in England, and he's awfully rich. Mamma thinks he will bring a valet with him."

"How did your family happen to know him?" inquired Betty, much interested.

"He and papa went to college together in England. He wasn't a lord then, though; he only got to be one about a year ago, papa says, because his uncle and his cousin, who were lords, both died, and he inherited the title."

"Just like Little Lord Fauntleroy," said Winifred; "I wonder if he minded it the way Fauntleroy did at first."

"Of course not," said Lulu, with superior wisdom. "Fauntleroy was only a silly little boy. I guess every man would like to be a lord if he had the chance. He and papa were great friends at college, and papa says he used to be very jolly and full of fun. I think he must really be rather nice, for when I asked papa whether I should say 'my lord' or 'your lordship' when I spoke to him, he only laughed, and said he didn't believe it would make much difference. I always thought a lord would be very angry if people didn't say 'my lord' or 'your lordship' whenever they spoke to him."

"Perhaps it's because he's such a new one that he isn't so very particular," Winifred suggested. "What made him come over to this country?"

"I don't know; I suppose because he wants to see it. He cruises about in his yacht, and mamma doesn't think he will stay very long with us, though she hopes he will on account of papa's being so fond of him. I hope he won't make a very long visit, for I suppose it can't help being rather solemn having a lord in the house."

"Lords in books are just like other people," Betty remarked practically. "Perhaps you'll like him ever so much, and be sorry when he goes away."

"I hope I shall see him," observed Jack, with unusual animation.

"What for?" inquired Betty, with some scorn. "I don't believe he looks a bit different from any one else."

"Well, we're English, you know," Jack explained, "and I should like to see a real English nobleman. It would be the next best thing to seeing the queen."

"I don't think I should be so very anxious to see the queen," declared democratic Betty. "I don't believe she's any different looking from other old ladies."

"Mother says we're subjects of the queen," Jack maintained, "and ought to love her, and you know if you have to love a person you would naturally like to see her. I don't know whether we have to love lords or not, but I should like to see one any way."

"There's mother on the bluff," said Winifred. "She's beckoning to us; I guess it must be time to go in."

The children scrambled hastily to their feet, Jack was helped into the go-cart, and the little party started in a homeward direction.

"Oh, mother, dear, we've had a lovely time this morning," exclaimed Winifred enthusiastically, as they joined Mrs. Hamilton on the bluff, "and Lulu has asked us all over to her house this afternoon. Her aunt is going to tell us stories."

"That will be very nice," said Mrs. Hamilton, smiling. "One of the ladies at the hotel has asked me to drive with her this afternoon, and I was rather doubtful about leaving you at home alone, but if Miss Warren wants you it will be all right."

"Mamma has gone to New York," Lulu explained, "but Aunt Daisy wants them all. I must run home now, for it's nearly one. Be sure you all come by half-past three. I have to do my lessons right after lunch, but I shall be all through by then."

"Jack and I have to do some lessons too," said Betty, "but we'll be at your house by half-past three. We'll stop for you, Winifred, as we pass the hotel."

Mrs. Randall was standing on the piazza of the boarding-house as Betty and Jack approached, and her tired face brightened wonderfully at sight of the two children. Betty was pushing the go-cart, and Jack waved his hand joyfully to his mother. Both little faces were radiant.

"Aren't you back earlier than usual, mother?" Betty asked, as they went into the house together, Jack moving slowly and cautiously on his crutches, but walking as neither his mother or Betty had ever expected to see him walk.

"Yes, rather earlier. Miss Leroy was going to a luncheon, and didn't take her full time. I shall be busy all the afternoon until six o'clock, though, for I begin with two new pupils to-day."

"Lulu Bell has asked us over to her house," said Betty; "her aunt is going to tell us stories. You don't mind our going, do you?"

"Oh, no, indeed, only don't tire poor Miss Warren out telling you stories, and if you get home before six, you may take Jack down on the beach for a little while. Dr. Bell wants him to be in the open air as much as possible."

"Mother," said Jack suddenly, as his mother was making him comfortable in the big wicker armchair by the window of their pleasant room on the ground floor, "did you ever see a lord when you were in England?"

"I think I have seen several in my life," said Mrs. Randall, smiling; "why do you want to know?"

"Because one is coming to stay at Lulu Bell's house, and I want to see him very much."

"Lords don't look any different from other people, do they, mother?" questioned Betty.

"Not in the least. I have an uncle who is a lord."

Mrs. Randall spoke rather absently, as though she were thinking of something else, but the astonished exclamations from both children quickly recalled her thoughts.

"You haven't really, have you, mother?" gasped Jack. Betty's eyes grew big and round with astonishment.

"Yes, my father's older brother was a lord, or is one if he is still alive. We never knew him very well, for his place was in a different county, and he and your grandfather were not good friends. I don't want you to mention this to any one, though," she added, flushing; "it would sound like bragging, and you know it is never right to do that."

"I always knew we had ancestors," said Betty thoughtfully, "but I never supposed any of them were lords. Is that the reason why you hate to accept things from people, mother?"

"I scarcely think that has much to do with it," Mrs. Randall said, laughing in spite of herself.

"Is your lord uncle in England now, mother?" Jack asked.

"I suppose so if he is still alive. He must be a very old man now, for he was several years older than your grandfather."

"And if he is dead, who is the lord now?"

"The title would naturally descend to his only son, my cousin. I never saw him, but I remember hearing that he was a rather promising boy. There is the bell for luncheon. Remember, children, you are not to mention this subject to any one, not even to Winifred or Lulu. I shall be displeased with you if you do."

Both children promised readily, but all through luncheon they were unusually silent, and when they had gone back to their room, and Mrs. Randall had started out on her afternoon rounds, Jack remarked suddenly, as he was turning over the pages in his English history:

"Now, Betty, you know the kind of lady I want you to be. I don't believe lords' relations ever work; not the lady relations, I mean, of course the men do."

"I don't see any use in being related to people if we don't even know them," said Betty, a little discontentedly. "Anyhow, I don't want to think about it, because if I do I shall forget and tell people, and then mother will be displeased. I don't care anything about lords, but if we could find Uncle Jack, that's what I should like."

"Don't you think mother might write to him some time?" Jack inquired wistfully.

"I know she won't, not unless she should be ill again, and I don't want that to happen. Now let's hurry and do our lessons, or we sha'n't be through in time to go to Lulu's house with Winifred."

CHAPTER XII

DRIFTING

Lulu was standing on the piazza, as the three other children approached the Bells' cottage, Winifred pushing the go-cart this time, and Betty holding a parasol over Jack's head. Instead of calling out a cheerful greeting as usual, however, she ran hastily and silently down the steps, and met them halfway across the lawn.

"We mustn't make any more noise than we can help," she said softly. "Poor Aunt Daisy has a dreadful headache. It came on all of a sudden, and she's gone to lie down. She says it may go away by and by if she can get a nap. Her room is right over the piazza, so we mustn't disturb her."

The children all expressed their sympathy and regret.

"Shall we go down on the beach and play?" Betty suggested.

Lulu looked doubtful.

"It's pretty hot down there," she objected, "and besides, we were there all the morning. We might go for a drive, only Thomas is so fussy, he never will harness the horses unless somebody grown up tells him to. Jane's ironing, so she can't take us anywhere. I'll tell you what we might do though"—with a sudden inspiration—"we might go down to the river and play shipwreck. That old boat that's fastened to the dock is just great to play shipwreck in. It's quite easy to get into it, even Jack could manage it all right, and I'd bring one of the cushions off the piazza to make him comfortable."

"Are you sure it's quite safe?" inquired cautious Betty, looking doubtful.

"Oh, yes, it's all right. We were in it the day the Rossiters were here, and papa saw us. It's fastened to the dock by a chain. Nothing could possibly happen. Come along; it's lovely and cool down there by the river, and if we stay here we shall be sure to forget and talk loud, and that will disturb Aunt Daisy."

"Oughtn't we ask some one first?" Winifred suggested.

"There isn't any one to ask. Papa and mamma are in New York, and Aunt Daisy's asleep. Jane wouldn't know, and she always makes a fuss about things she doesn't understand. If it hadn't been all right, papa would have said so when the Rossiters were here."

This seemed a practical argument, and although Betty still felt a little uncomfortable about the wisdom of the proceeding, she made no further objections, and five minutes later the little party were standing on the dock. It was, as Lulu had said, very easy to step into the old rowboat, which, indeed, looked safe enough even to Betty, being fastened to the dock by a long chain. With a little help from the girls, Jack succeeded in crawling over the side, and was made comfortable in the stern, while the others settled themselves on the benches.

"Isn't it perfectly lovely here?" cried the little boy enthusiastically, dabbling his hands in the cool water. "I was never in a boat like this before."

"Of course it's lovely," said Lulu in a tone of unqualified satisfaction; "I told you it would be. It's much nicer than on that hot piazza, or on the beach either."

"There are mosquitoes," Winifred remarked, flapping vigorously about her head with her handkerchief. "Mosquitoes always do bite me most dreadfully."

"That's because you're so sweet," said Lulu. "Try not to think about them, and then you won't mind. Aunt Daisy says if only people wouldn't think about disagreeable things, they would be a great deal happier."

"Look, look; I can make the boat rock," cried the excited Jack.

"Oh, isn't it fun?"

"Now," said Lulu, as usual taking the initiative; "we are a party of shipwrecked people, escaping in a lifeboat from a sinking ship. We are away out in the middle of the ocean. All the other people in the ship have been drowned, and we have escaped in the only boat there was. I am a widow lady traveling with my little boy. You are my little boy, Jack, and you are very ill. You must put your head in my lap, and keep your eyes shut as if you were suffering a great deal. Winifred is our faithful maid, who has been everywhere with us, and has divided her last ship biscuit with us."

"And what am I?" inquired Betty, beginning to enter the spirit of the new game. "Don't make the boat rock quite so hard, Jack, dear, please."

"You are the kind old sailor, who has saved us all. Some bad men on the ship wanted to take this lifeboat, and leave us to drown, but you shot them all down, and now you are taking us to an inhabited island you know about. We have been three days without food, and without seeing a sail, but I have promised that if you will bring us safely to land I will make you very rich."

"Are you very rich yourself?" inquired Betty.

"Of course, I'm a very great lady. No, I think I will be a princess; that will be nicer, and when people do brave things I make them my knights."

"But there aren't any knights now," Winifred objected.

"Well, then, it isn't now; it's a long time ago, about the time of Queen Elizabeth, I guess. Now come on, let's begin."

The next half-hour was one of the most delightfully exciting periods the children had ever enjoyed. Lulu's vivid imagination carried them all along with it, and even practical Betty forgot everything else in the interest of the shipwreck. Jack played the suffering child to perfection; moaned pitiously, and implored his mother in feeble whispers for a crust of bread or a drop of water. The food was all gone, Lulu said, but Winifred endeavored to procure the desired water by dipping her hands in the river, and splashing salt water over Jack's face. Some of it ran into his eyes, which was not pleasant, but Jack was too polite to complain. Betty spoke words of encouragement and cheer, while she scanned the horizon through an imaginary telescope. Lulu hung over her suffering child, soothing his woes by the tenderest caresses and promising innumerable purses filled with gold to Betty and Winifred, as rewards for their faithful services, if ever they should reach the shore alive.

"There's a dreadful storm coming up," announced Lulu, suddenly glancing up at the cloudless blue sky, and beginning to wave her arms frantically. "We shall be drowned, I know we shall. Make the boat rock as much as you can, Betty, so it will seem as if the sea was getting rough. Oh, what will become of us? Do you think we shall all perish, sailor?"

"Can't say; hope not," said Betty, who had an idea that all sailors spoke in short, jerky sentences.

"You'll save us if you possibly can, won't you?" said Winifred, who was playing so hard that she was almost frightened.

"Will if I can," returned Betty in the deepest growl she could assume.

"Oh, Lulu, please let us see a sail pretty soon," urged Jack. "I'm getting so tired of keeping my eyes shut, and it seems so dreadfully real."

"There aren't any oars, and we're drifting."

"Oh, yes, we shall see one before long," said Lulu reassuringly. "It'll come just at the last awful moment; it always does in books."

At that moment a sudden burst of sunshine dazzled all their eyes.

"Why, how funny," exclaimed Betty, forgetting her nautical manner, and speaking in her natural voice; "I wonder what makes it sunny all at once. It was nice and shady a minute ago."

A shrill scream from Winifred brought Betty's wonder to an abrupt end.

"Look, oh look!" shrieked the little girl, pointing with a shaking finger towards the shore; "the boat's moving, it's moving all by itself."

Every one followed the direction of Winifred's terrified gaze. Sure enough; several feet of water already separated the boat from the shore.

"The chain's broken," gasped Betty, growing very white. "It must have broken when we made the boat rock so hard. There aren't any oars, and we're drifting. Oh, what shall we do?"

Winifred began to cry.

"It's all your fault, Lulu," she wailed; "you said it was safe, and now we shall be drowned, and what will mother do. Oh, oh, oh!"

Lulu was shaking from head to foot, but realizing the truth of her friend's accusation, she made an effort to think of some way of escape.

"Couldn't we jump out and wade ashore?" she suggested desperately.

"Of course not," said Betty, with prompt decision; "we don't know how deep the water is, and besides we couldn't leave Jack."

Poor little Jack lifted his white face from his sister's shoulder, where he had hidden it in the first moment of terror. His eyes were big with fright, and his lips trembled pitifully.

"Never mind about me," he faltered. "Maybe if you get ashore you can send some one after me. I'm a boy, you know; I ought to be able to take care of myself."

"You're the bravest boy I ever knew," sobbed impulsive Lulu, throwing her arms around Jack's neck, "and we wouldn't leave you for the whole world, would we, girls?"

"Of course we wouldn't," said Winifred emphatically. Betty said nothing, but hugged her brother tight in wordless love and admiration.

"We sha'n't be drowned, any way, I know we sha'n't," said Lulu, her courage beginning to rise. "There are so many boats on the river that some one will be sure to see us pretty soon."

"There's a man over there fishing on that dock," cried Winifred hopefully. "He isn't looking this way, but maybe if we shout very loud he'll hear us."

The four little voices were accordingly raised, and shout succeeded shout till the opposite bank sent back the echoes, but the fisherman never turned his head. Perhaps he was deaf, or possibly he was accustomed to hear children shouting in that way, merely for the sake of amusement. Not another human being was in sight.

"He won't see us, oh, he won't look," moaned Winifred, once more beginning to cry. "See how far away from the shore we are getting. Oh, we shall be drowned, I know we shall."

Betty and Lulu had also noticed how fast the boat was drifting.

"The tide's going out," whispered Betty, with white lips. "Where does this river go to, Lulu?"

"Into the ocean, I think," said Lulu, shivering. "It has to go round Sandy Hook first, though," she added more hopefully, "and somebody will be sure to see us before we get there."

"Are you very frightened, Jack, dear?" Betty whispered, nestling close to her little brother.

"N—no, not so very," returned Jack tremulously; "only—only, if anything does happen think how unhappy mother will be, and—and, I did hope I should be able to walk just like other people."

This was too much for Betty, and she promptly burst into tears.

"Oh, we must do something, we must," cried Lulu, almost beside herself with anxiety. "It's all my fault, I know, but I really did think it was safe. I didn't mean to be naughty, I truly didn't, Winifred."

"I know you didn't," sobbed Winifred, hugging her friend in a burst of remorse. "I didn't mean what I said, not a single word of it, only I was so dreadfully frightened."

"Perhaps if we keep on shouting all the time, and waving our handkerchiefs, some one will notice us," Betty suggested.

This seemed a good idea, and was promptly acted upon, but though they shouted till their throats were sore, and waved till their arms ached, no friendly face appeared, and faster and faster drifted the little boat away from home and friends.

"I wonder what time it is," said Winifred, when they had at last left off shouting, in order to gain a little breath. "It seems as if we had been out on the river for hours and hours."

"We can't have been as long as that," said Betty, "because the sun is just as bright as it was when we started. I guess the time seems longer than it really is."

"I wonder where our mothers are now," remarked Lulu mournfully. "Mine must be on the boat coming home from the city."

"And mine is driving with Mrs. Martin," said Winifred. "Oh, what will they all do when they get home and we're not there." The picture called up by this remark was too dreadful to be borne with fortitude, and all four children simultaneously burst into tears.

Suddenly Jack's voice broke in upon the wails of the three little girls.

"Look, oh, look! there's a steamboat; it's coming this way."

Every eye was turned in the direction Jack pointed. Sure enough, a large steam yacht was coming rapidly down the river, her head pointed straight towards them.

"Wave, keep waving as hard as you can," cried Betty excitedly. "Let's all shout together again, and perhaps they'll hear us."

"Wait till they get a little nearer, they couldn't hear us yet," advised Jack. "Oh, do you really think they'll save us?"

"Of course they will," said Lulu confidently. "Oh, look, look, they see us already; there's a man waving back to us. Maybe they think we're only doing it for fun. How shall we let them know we want them to help us?"

"We must shout," said Betty, and she set the example by raising her voice to its highest pitch.

"Please, please help us! Our boat's drifting, and we haven't got any oars. Oh, please, do come and help us!"

"They understand us!" cried Lulu joyfully. "See, the man's nodding his head. Why, they're stopping! Oh, don't you believe they're going to help us after all?"

For the next few moments the children waited in breathless suspense, almost too excited to speak. Then Jack announced:

"They're getting into a rowboat. See those two men? That's the one that nodded to us; I guess he's the captain. Let's shout again."

So again the four little voices were raised in agonized appeal, and this time there came an answering shout from the other boat.

"Don't be frightened, children, you're all right. We're coming to you as fast as we can."

The wind brought the cheery, encouraging words straight across the water to the terrified children, and oh! the relief of that comforting assurance to each wildly beating little heart. The men in the boat rowed fast, and soon the splash of approaching oars was heard. Lulu and Winifred began to cry again, but it was for joy this time, not sorrow. Betty and Jack clung to each other in speechless relief. In a few moments the two boats were side by side; a rope was thrown securely around the oarless craft, and the children were safe.

"And now, my little friends, you must let us take you on board the yacht," said the man whom Jack had concluded to be the captain.

He was a tall, broad-shouldered man, with a rather handsome face, and it seemed to the children as though his cheery voice was the pleasantest sound they had ever heard in their lives. He and his companion—who appeared to be one of the sailors—began at once rowing back towards the yacht, keeping the children's boat in tow. A sudden fit of shyness had fallen upon the party, and nobody spoke until the stranger inquired, regarding the solemn little faces rather quizzically:

"How did it happen?"

"We were playing in the boat," Betty explained. "It was fastened to the dock, and we thought it was safe. The chain broke and we hadn't any oars."

"Have you been drifting long? Were you very much frightened?"

"It seemed like a long time," said Betty, "and we were pretty frightened. It was very kind of you to come and help us."

The gentleman smiled. He was a gentleman, the children all felt sure of that, and Lulu afterwards remarked that he had the most beautiful smile she had ever seen.

Nothing more was said until they reached the side of the yacht. Several men, evidently members of the crew, were standing on the deck, watching with interest the approach of the two boats.

"Now," said the gentleman, rising, "do you think you can manage to climb this ladder? It's perfectly safe, and I will help you."

Lulu and Winifred rose promptly, but Betty remained seated, her arm around her little brother.

"Don't be afraid," said the gentleman encouragingly; "it's quite easy."

"Oh, I'm not afraid," said Betty, her lip beginning to quiver, "but I can't leave my brother. He can't climb. He has always been a cripple until this summer, and he's only just beginning to walk now. We'll have to stay here till we get to the landing."

While Betty was speaking the stranger's face had softened wonderfully, and he looked at Jack with an expression of increased interest. Without a word he stepped to the side of his own boat, and, leaning over, lifted the little boy in his arms.

"Now I fancy we can manage it, my little man," he said kindly, and in another moment he had lifted Jack up to one of the men on the yacht, who in turn had placed the child in safety on the deck. The little girls were then carefully helped up the ladder, and in less than three minutes the whole party was standing, safe and dry, on the deck of what they afterwards learned to be one of the finest steam yachts in the world.

"And now I shall have to take you all as far as the steamboat landing," said the stranger, as he placed Jack comfortably in a steamer chair. "It will not take more than half an hour, and from there we can easily send word to your friends. Where do you live, by the way?"

"We live at Navesink," said Lulu, suddenly recovering her speech and her manners now that the danger was over, and remembering all at once that she had always been considered a very polite little girl. "My papa has a cottage there, and the others all came over to spend the afternoon with me. It was my fault about the boat, but I thought it was safe. I think we must have made it rock too much when we were playing shipwreck."

"Very possibly," said the gentleman, who looked considerably amused by this explanation. "It is never a very wise plan to make boats rock too much. But now let me see"—glancing at his watch—"it is only a little after five, and we shall be at the landing by half-past. Do you think your friends will be very much frightened about you?"

"I don't think so," said Lulu. "My mother has gone to the city for the day; Winifred's mother is out driving, and Betty and Jack say their mother told them they needn't come home before six. My papa has a telephone, and we can let them know as soon as we get to the landing."

"Not at all a bad idea, and in the meantime won't you make yourselves at home on board my yacht? By the way, I think shipwrecked people are apt to be hungry."

"We are not very hungry, thank you," said Lulu politely; "you see, we didn't start until half-past three."

The stranger smiled again, and said something in a low tone to the steward, who immediately disappeared.

"We've none of us ever been on a yacht before," said Lulu, feeling that it was her duty to keep up the conversation, as none of the others seemed inclined to talk. "I think it's a very nice place."

"I have crossed the Atlantic in this yacht," the gentleman said pleasantly.

"Have you really?" exclaimed Lulu, looking very much surprised. "I didn't know people ever did that, except perhaps lords."

"And why lords in particular?" the stranger inquired, smiling.

"I don't know, only a lord is coming to stay with us, and papa says he has crossed the ocean in his yacht."

"Indeed! and may I ask what your name is?"

"Lulu Bell. My father is Dr. Bell, and we live in New York in winter."

"Well, this is a coincidence, I declare," exclaimed the gentleman, looking really quite excited. "I had no idea that one of the children in that rowboat would prove to be the little daughter of my old friend. Have you ever heard your father speak of Lord Carresford?"

"Why, yes," said Lulu, her eyes opening wide in astonishment; "he's the lord that's coming to stay with us to-morrow."

"I am Lord Carresford," said the gentleman, laughing and holding out his hand.

"Children," gasped Lulu, turning to her three companions, who had been whispering together at a little distance from their rescuer and herself, and who had not paid much attention to the conversation, "oh, children, the very most wonderful thing has happened. This really is a lord's yacht, and this gentleman is—'His Lordship.'"

CHAPTER XIII

"HIS LORDSHIP"

Before the children had fully recovered from the amazement caused by Lulu's announcement the steward reappeared bearing a tray containing lemonade and cake, and Lord Carresford requested them to take some refreshments. Although not in a starving condition, they were all blessed with healthy appetites, and the cake and lemonade disappeared very rapidly. While they ate their host talked to them, and he was so pleasant and merry, and, in fact, talked so much like any other gentleman, that Winifred whispered to Jack: "Betty was right, wasn't she? A lord isn't a bit different from anybody else," to which Jack replied, "No, only rather nicer than most people, don't you think so?"

By the time the impromptu repast was finished the yacht had reached the steamboat landing, and Lord Carresford hurried away to the telephone office to inform Dr. and Mrs. Bell of their little daughter's whereabouts. During his absence the steward—who appeared to be a very agreeable person—showed the children over the yacht, carrying Jack in his arms almost as tenderly and carefully as his master had done.

"I think a yacht is the most interesting place I have ever been in," Lulu informed "his lordship" on his return from the telephone office. "I should like very much indeed to cross the ocean in one. We went to Europe once, and I liked the steamer very much, but mamma and Aunt Daisy were seasick."

"If you please, sir," interrupted Betty—"I mean, your lordship—do you know whether our families have been very much worried about us?"

"I think not," said "his lordship," smiling kindly at the earnest little face. "Dr. Bell himself came to the telephone, and seemed greatly surprised to learn of the state of affairs. He and his wife have just returned from the city, and had not yet discovered that their little girl was missing. He says he will drive over to the landing for you at once."

Betty drew a long breath of relief.

"I'm so glad," she said; "I was afraid mother might be frightened. She was very ill last spring, and we shouldn't like to have her worried about anything."

After that Lord Carresford took them down into the cabin and showed them some interesting shells and other curious things which he had collected during his wanderings. He had been nearly all over the world, it seemed, and was certainly one of the most fascinating "grown-ups" the children had ever met. So the moments flew, and almost before any one could have believed such a thing possible, Dr. Bell arrived with the carriage. At sight of her father Lulu suddenly burst into tears again and flung herself impulsively into his arms.

"I wasn't naughty, papa, I really wasn't," she sobbed. "I did think the boat was safe or I wouldn't have asked the others in. Oh, papa, dear, you won't be angry, will you?"

"No, no, little woman," Dr. Bell said, kissing her. "I am only angry with myself for not having been more careful. If anything had happened—Jack, old fellow, how can I thank you?" And the doctor wrung Lord Carresford's hands in gratitude too deep for words.

The greeting between the two old friends was a very hearty one, and Dr. Bell would have insisted on Lord Carresford's returning with them at once to Navesink, but the latter explained that he had promised to dine with some friends at the Highlands that evening, and would consequently be unable to arrive at the Bells' before the following day. It was getting late, and as Dr. Bell was anxious to get his party home as soon as possible, the good-byes and thanks were quickly said and the four children were packed into the Bells' comfortable depot wagon. Lord Carresford insisted on carrying Jack to the carriage.

"Good-bye, my small friend," he said kindly, as he tucked the laprobe about the little boy's feet. "I shall see you again, I hope, when I come to Navesink."

"Good-bye, sir, and thank you very much," said Jack, holding out his hand. "I am very glad I met you. I have wanted for a long time to meet a lord, but I didn't really believe I ever should."

It was nearly eight o'clock before the party reached home, and Dr. Bell drove at once to the boarding-house to leave Betty and Jack. Mrs. Randall was standing on the piazza gazing anxiously out into the gathering dusk.

"Here we are, mother," called Betty, as the carriage drew up before the door; "we're all right, and I'm sure Jack hasn't taken cold."

Mrs. Randall hurried down the steps, and took Jack in her arms.

"Let me carry him," she said almost sharply to the doctor, who would have lifted the child from the carriage. "Oh, my little boy, were you very, very much frightened?"

"I was pretty frightened at first," Jack admitted, with his arms clasped tight around his mother's neck, "but afterwards, when the yacht came, and the lord was so kind, I liked it, and then it was a great comfort to know you weren't frightened about us."

"Are you sure you were warm enough all the time?" Mrs. Randall questioned anxiously.

"Oh, yes, as warm as toast," said Jack, laughing. "They wrapped me all up in the laprobe driving home—and see this pretty silk handkerchief. The lord tied it around my neck for fear I should be cold."

"The lord?" repeated Mrs. Randall, looking very much puzzled.

"Why, yes, the lord that owns the yacht—and isn't it funny, mother, he's the same lord that's coming to stay at Dr. Bell's. He said he hoped he should see me again, and I hope so too, for he is the nicest gentleman I ever met."

"Mother," said Jack an hour later, when his mother was putting him to bed, "do you know, I'm more glad than I ever was before that I'm an English boy."

"Why?" his mother asked, smiling.

"Because when I grow up I shall be an Englishman, and I do think Englishmen are very splendid. I like Dr. Bell, and Mr. Hamilton, and a good many other American gentlemen, but I never saw any one quite so splendid as that lord."

Mrs. Randall laughed.

"You enthusiastic little hero worshiper," she said. "What was the lord's name, by the way?"

"I don't know," said Jack; "Lulu just called him 'your lordship.' They might have names like other people, I suppose."

"Yes, of course, and it isn't customary to address a lord as 'your lordship' either, at least not among people of our class."

"That must be why he laughed when Lulu did it," said Betty reflectively, "but she only wanted to be very respectful. Dr. Bell called him Jack."

"Betty," whispered Jack, when their mother had left the room, and the two children were alone together, "do you suppose we shall ever see Uncle Jack?"

"I don't know," said Betty sadly. "I'm sure mother never will write to him, and of course he wouldn't be likely to come to America."

"You don't know where he lives in England, do you?"

"Mother told me once, but I forget the name of the place. Why do you want to know?"

"Because," said Jack slowly, raising himself on his elbow as he spoke, "if I knew it, I think I would write him a letter myself."

"Oh, Jack, you wouldn't dare?"

"Yes, I think I would," said Jack, "and I think if he really came, mother would love it."

"She would love to see him," Betty admitted, "but she doesn't like to write, for fear he might think she wanted money or something like that."

"I want to see him too," said Jack; "I want it very much indeed."

"Why? You never seemed to care so much before."

"No, I didn't, not till to-day, but then you see I had never talked to an Englishman before."

"And does that make a difference?" Betty asked, somewhat puzzled.

"Of course it does. Uncle Jack is an Englishman too, and perhaps—I don't really suppose he is—but he might be just a little bit like the lord."

"You are a funny boy," said Betty, laughing. "The lord was very kind, and ever so good to us, but then——"

"He was the most splendid man I ever saw," interrupted Jack, "and I wish—I do wish—that when I grow up I might be just exactly like him."

The Randalls was not the only household in which Lord Carresford was the subject of conversation that evening.

"Your friend has certainly succeeded in captivating the children's affections, Charlie," said Mrs. Bell to her husband, as she joined him and her sister on the piazza after having seen Lulu safely tucked up in bed. "Lulu has talked of nothing else since she came home, and I have just been talking to Mrs. Hamilton at the telephone. She says her little girl is of the opinion that 'his lordship' is the most delightful person she has ever encountered."

"That was always the way with old Jack," said the doctor, smiling. "There was never a man, woman, or child who had not something to say in his praise. He was the most popular man in his class."

"I declare I can hardly wait till to-morrow to make his acquaintance," laughed Miss Warren. "Did you ever know any of his people, Charlie?"

"No, I never met any of them. I fancy his father was a rather eccentric old gentleman, who did not encourage visitors. There was a sister he used to talk about a good deal, but I never met her. I left college the year before he did, and I have a vague recollection of having heard that the sister made an unfortunate marriage, but I have forgotten the circumstances."

"I hope that poor little Randall boy won't be any the worse for his adventure of this afternoon," Mrs. Bell said, a little anxiously.

"Oh, no, I think not; we wrapped him up well coming home, and he seemed as happy as possible. Indeed, I have an idea that he rather enjoyed the whole adventure, for he is a true boy, after all."

"I like Mrs. Randall very much," remarked Miss Warren. "She is an excellent teacher, and a thoroughly cultivated woman. I wish I knew more of her history, and could do something to help her, for I am sure she has had a hard time. Don't you know anything about her family, Charlie?"

"Nothing whatever. Betty once told me that their only relative is an uncle in England, whom she has never seen."

"Lulu says Jack's grandfather was a general," said Mrs. Bell. "They are certainly a most interesting family, and I wish we could manage to do something for that poor Mrs. Randall. There is a tragedy of some kind written plainly on her face."

CHAPTER XIV

JACK'S NEW FRIEND

"May I inquire what you are thinking of so intently, Miss Lulu?"

Lulu gave a little start, and glanced up from her seat on the piazza steps, into Lord Carresford's kind, amused face. "His lordship," stretched comfortably in the hammock, with book and cigar, had been regarding her in silence for several minutes.

"I was thinking," said Lulu slowly, "how differently things generally happen from the way you expect them to."

"I thought it must be something rather absorbing," said "his lordship" with a smile, "you looked so very serious. What has put that particular thought into your head just now, I wonder."

"Why, it was you," said Lulu, flushing a little. "I began by thinking how different you were from what we thought you were going to be. When papa said a lord was coming to stay with us, I was really quite uncomfortable. I thought it would be such a dreadfully solemn thing to have one in the house."

Lord Carresford laughed.

"And you have since discovered that I am not such a very solemn person after all, is that it?"

"Yes," said Lulu; "you're not the least bit solemn, you know, but much nicer than any other gentleman who ever came to stay with us. It's only two days since you came, but it seems as if we'd all known you a long time. Betty said she didn't believe lords were any different from other people, but the rest of us all thought they must be."

"Good for Betty. How did she obtain her superior knowledge about lords?"

"She said the lords in books were just like other people, and then I suppose being English made her know a little more about such things, though she's never been in England herself."

"English," repeated Lord Carresford in surprise; "I did not know that the Hamiltons were English."

"They're not, but Betty isn't Mrs. Hamilton's little girl. Did you think she was Winifred's sister?"

"Yes, I did think so; and the little lame boy—isn't he a Hamilton either?"

"Oh, no," said Lulu, laughing; "Winifred hasn't any brothers or sisters at all. She and I are great friends, but we haven't known Betty and Jack very long. They lived in the same apartment house with Winifred in New York, and she got acquainted with them in the spring. Their mother was very ill, and papa attended her. Jack couldn't walk at all then, but papa thought he might be cured, so he went to a hospital, and had an operation. They came down here, because papa thought the sea air would do Jack good. They're staying at Mrs. Wilson's boarding house, and their mother gives music lessons. We're growing very fond of Betty and Jack, and I mean to have them for my friends always."

"I took quite a fancy to Jack myself," said Lord Carresford; "he struck me as a rather remarkable little fellow."

Lulu's face brightened.

"I'm very glad," she said, "because Jack is so anxious to know you. Betty says he thinks you are the loveliest gentleman he has ever seen. He talks about you all the time and when he and Betty came over here yesterday, and I told him you had gone driving with papa, he looked dreadfully disappointed."

Lord Carresford seemed both pleased and amused.

"I must make a point of looking up my young friend, and having a little talk with him then," he said. "Do you suppose he is to be found on the beach this afternoon?"

"Yes, I know he is; I saw Betty wheeling him down a little while ago. I'm waiting for Winifred, and then we're going too. I suppose you wouldn't care to go with us? It's very nice and cool down there."

"I think I should like it very much," said Lord Carresford, smiling. "Your father will not be at home before six, I believe."

"No, and mamma and Aunt Daisy have gone to a tea. Don't you like teas, Lord Carresford?"

"Not very much. I prefer sitting here and watching the ocean. Do you enjoy teas yourself?"

"I think I should like them," said Lulu reflectively; "I like most grown-up things. Betty says she wants to be a housekeeper when she grows up, but I should much rather be an authoress. Aunt Daisy is an authoress, you know, and people always like to talk to her. Jack is going to be an artist when he grows up, and he doesn't want Betty to be a housekeeper, because he says English ladies never work. Jack is really a very unselfish little boy. That day in the boat he wanted us all to wade ashore and leave him alone. He said he was a boy, and ought to be able to take care of himself. We think him very brave, and papa calls him a little soldier. Oh, here comes Winifred." And Lulu sprang to her feet, and hurried across the lawn to greet her friend.

Winifred was very much impressed when her friend informed her in a whisper that "his lordship" was actually going to the beach with them, and the three were soon on their way.

"Lord Carresford," said Lulu rather timidly, as they passed out of the gate, and turned in the direction of the board walk, "would you mind very much if I asked you a question?"

"Not in the least."

"Do you like being a lord?"

"Well, I can scarcely say that I dislike it," said "his lordship," laughing. "The fact is, I don't think I have quite recovered from the surprise of the whole thing as yet."

"Why were you surprised? Didn't you always expect to be one?"

"I never even dreamed of such a thing until about a year ago. My uncle was Lord Carresford as long as he lived, and when he died the title naturally descended to his son, my cousin. He had always been very strong and well, but he died suddenly of pneumonia a year ago last spring, and as he was not married, and I was the nearest male relative, the title and estates came to me."

"That's just the way it was with little Lord Fauntleroy," said Winifred, much struck by the coincidence, "and he didn't think he was going to like it at first, but afterwards he didn't mind so much. Have you got a beautiful castle in England, like the one Fauntleroy had?"

"I have several rather nice places. If you ever come to England you must make me a visit at Carresford Towers. You would like that, I think; it is very pretty."

"We should like it very much," said Winifred politely. "I wish Jack could go to England some time; he's so much interested in all English things. Have you got a park with deer in it?"

"Yes, a very nice one."

"And who will be Lord Carresford when you—after you get through?" Lulu inquired, finding some difficulty in framing her question in the most delicate manner.

Lord Carresford laughed.

"That depends upon circumstances," he said. "If I should happen to marry and have a son, he would naturally take my place. Otherwise the title would go to one of my nephews, if I had any."

"Have you got any nephews now?" Lulu asked.

"No, at least none that I know of. I have two married sisters in England, but their children all happen to be girls."

"It's all very interesting," said Lulu; "it sounds just like a thing out of a book. There are Betty and Jack sitting on the bathing house steps. Won't they be surprised when they see who is with us?"

"Well, my boy, and how have you been amusing yourself to-day?" Lord Carresford asked kindly, seating himself beside Jack on the steps, as the three little girls strolled away in search of other amusements.

"I've been having a very pleasant time, sir," said Jack, whose heart was beating faster than was quite comfortable, and whose cheeks were flushing and paling by turns. To find himself actually alone with "the lord," engaged in familiar conversation with him, was an honor he had never even dreamed of. "Betty and I were on the beach all the morning. I like it better than any other place."

"You are fond of the sea, then?"

"Oh, yes, indeed, I love just to sit and look at it. It's very interesting to look at things, don't you think so?"

"Well, yes, I suppose it is, though I can't say I have ever thought very much on the subject."

"Well, you see, it's rather different with me," Jack explained in his odd, old-fashioned way, "because until this summer I never saw many things. I hardly ever went out, and you know one can't see very much from back windows, especially when one lives on the top floor."

"I should not imagine the view could have been very interesting," said Lord Carresford, smiling; "but how did it happen that you so seldom went out?"

"Why, you see, I was too heavy to carry, and of course we couldn't afford to have a carriage. I did go in a carriage once, though; I saw Central Park." And Jack launched forth into a description of Winifred's invitation, and his birthday treat. Lord Carresford began to look really interested.

"And how did you amuse yourself all day in the house?" he inquired, rather curiously, when Jack had finished his story.

"Oh, I got on very well. I read a good deal, and drew pictures, and then Betty was always there, and mother came home in the afternoons. You never heard my mother play on the piano, did you?"

"No, I have never had the pleasure of meeting your mother."

"I think she plays better than any one else in the world," said Jack simply. "She used to play for me every evening, because she knew I loved it, though sometimes she was dreadfully tired. Oh, I had very good times, though of course it is much nicer here."

"Did you say you drew pictures?" Lord Carresford asked.

"Yes, I like to draw better than almost anything else, but I don't suppose I do it at all right. I've been making a picture this afternoon."

"May I look at it? I am very much interested in pictures."

Jack produced a folded paper from his pocket, which he handed to Lord Carresford.

"I was going to take it home to mother," he explained; "she likes to keep all my pictures."

Lord Carresford unfolded the paper, and glanced, at first rather carelessly, at the rough little sketch. Then suddenly his expression changed, and when he again turned to the little boy there was a new interest in his manner.

"It is very good," said Lord Carresford.—*Page* .

"Who taught you to draw?" he asked rather abruptly.

"No one," said Jack; "I just did it. My father was an artist, and mother thinks that may be the reason why I can do it. Please, sir, would you mind telling me if it's very bad?"

"It is very good," said Lord Carresford heartily; "remarkably good for a boy of your age. You will be an artist when you grow up, or I am much mistaken."

Jack's face was radiant.

"Do you really think so?" he asked breathlessly. "Oh, I'm so glad. I should like so very, very much to be an artist."

"Why are you so anxious on the subject?" Lord Carresford asked, with a kindly glance at the flushed, eager little face.

"I think it's partly because my father was one, but mostly because I want to make money," said Jack.

"You want to make money, eh? and what will you do with the money when it is made?"

"Why, take care of mother and Betty, of course," said Jack, surprised at the question. "Isn't that what men always do with the money they make?—take care of their families, I mean."

"Well, I am afraid not always," said Lord Carresford, laughing; "don't you think that you may need a share for yourself?"

"Oh, not much," said Jack confidently. "You see, I shall always live with mother and Betty, and if they have things, why, of course I shall have them too. I don't want mother to give music lessons when I grow up, and Betty mustn't be a housekeeper, though she says she would like to be one."

"Have you a particular objection to housekeepers, then?"

"Oh, no, it isn't that, only I don't think—Lord Carresford, would you mind telling me something?"

"Not at all; what is it?"

"It's about ladies," said Jack, flushing; "English ladies I mean. They never work, do they?"

"Many of them do when it is necessary. There is nothing to be ashamed of in honest work, you know."

"Oh, I know there isn't. Mother works, and Lulu's aunt writes books. But I mean the kind of ladies who have lords for their relations—do they ever work?"

"Well, they are not very often obliged to, but I have known of cases where even ladies of title have supported themselves. I see your point, though; you don't want your sister to be obliged to work."

"No," said Jack; "not if I can take care of her. I want her to live in a beautiful place, with a park, like mother—I mean like some people—and never have to do anything she doesn't want to."

"Well," said Lord Carresford, smiling, "I am not certain about the park, but you ought to be able to make a comfortable home for your mother and sister. You have talent, my boy, and it should be cultivated. You must have lessons."

Jack's bright face clouded.

"Don't lessons cost a good deal, sir?" he asked anxiously.

"Yes, but in a case like yours I don't think the expense of the thing should be taken into consideration. A boy who can draw as well as you can without ever taking a lesson, ought to have every advantage for improving his talent. Your mother should place you under one of the very best teachers in New York, and then when you are older you will be able to make good use of the advantages you have received."

"But if it costs a good deal of money I'm afraid mother couldn't possibly afford it," said Jack mournfully. "I shouldn't like to speak to her about it either, because it might worry her. When mother's worried about things she doesn't sleep, and then her eyes look so tired."

Lord Carresford was silent. There was something rather pathetic in the sight of the little patient face, that but a moment before had been so bright and hopeful. This small boy was interesting him very much. He thought of his own great wealth, and of how easy it would be to him to give the child the help he needed. And yet, as he told himself, it would not do to be too hasty. He really knew nothing whatever about this family. So when he spoke again, it was on a different subject.

The little girls soon returned, and Lulu requested Lord Carresford to tell them a story. "His lordship's" powers in that direction had already been discovered by the little girl. He complied very willingly with the request, and soon had the whole party listening in breathless interest to an account of some of his experiences when hunting big game in India. So Dr. Bell, coming down to the beach on his return from town, found a very happy little group gathered about his friend, and it was not without considerable regret that the children bade good-bye to their fascinating entertainer, and watched him and the doctor walking away together.

"That little boy interests me very much," Lord Carresford remarked, pausing to light a cigar, when they had reached the board walk, "and do you know that he has a great deal of talent?"

"Talent for what?" the doctor inquired in surprise.

"Have you never happened to see any of his sketches?"

"No, never; are they worth anything?"

"My dear fellow, the child is a genius. He tells me he has never had a drawing lesson in his life, and yet, I assure you, his drawings are better than many I have seen made by students who have been at work for years. He ought to have the best teaching that can be procured."

Dr. Bell looked interested.

"I am afraid there may be difficulties in the way," he said. "The mother is a music teacher, and I am sorry to say is far from strong. I fancy she has a rather uphill road to travel."

"Well, she ought to be told of her boy's talent at any rate," said Lord Carresford, rather impatiently. "The raising of sufficient money for lessons ought not to be difficult. I am sure I should be very glad to contribute myself to so good a cause."

"It might not be difficult in some cases," said the doctor, laughing, "but I am afraid that in that particular case there would be a good deal of trouble. The mother has the airs and manner of a queen. I should like to see her expression if any one were to propose to her that a fund should be raised in order to give her small boy drawing lessons. I have never yet been able to muster sufficient courage to explain to her that I do not intend sending in a bill for professional services. She was laid up with a sharp attack of pneumonia this spring. When she was taken ill she told her children she could not afford to have a doctor sent for. Fortunately Hamilton's little girl, who happened to be a friend of theirs, took matters into her own hands, in the absence of her mother, and came for me. The poor woman was delirious when I reached there, and we had a hard time to pull her through. I believe that if it were not for the children she would starve rather than accept a penny from any one. She adores them, though, especially the boy, and no wonder, for he is one of the finest little fellows I have ever seen."

"Poor soul," said Lord Carresford, with a sigh. "Well, she must be told of her boy's prospects, and then she can do as she likes about accepting the necessary aid."

CHAPTER XV

SOMETHING HAPPENS

"Is it finished, Winifred?"

"Ye—yes," said Winifred slowly, laying down her pencil, and surveying rather ruefully the large sheet of foolscap in her lap. "It's finished, but it isn't any good; I know your aunt won't like it."

"Oh, yes, she will," said Lulu encouragingly, coming over to her friend's side, and surveying the result of her labors with evident satisfaction. The two little girls were together in Lulu's room, and for the past half-hour Winifred had been making a desperate effort to finish her story.

"It isn't as long as mine," Lulu went on, "But I think it's a very pretty story. 'The Indian' is a nice name, isn't it? I've called mine 'The Discovery of New Haven.' Of course I don't mean the New Haven where the Boston trains stop. It's just an imaginary place, you know. We must go and read our stories to Aunt Daisy now. I'm just crazy to know how she will like them."

Winifred hesitated.

"I know she'll think mine dreadfully silly," she said. "Don't you think you could possibly read it to her after I go home?"

"Of course not," said Lulu with decision; "you must read it to her yourself, the same as I do. Come along."

Winifred rose rather reluctantly, and the two little girls went downstairs, and out on the piazza, where they found Lord Carresford and Miss Warren sitting together. "His lordship" was reading aloud to the blind lady, but at the children's approach he laid down his book.

"Well, young ladies," he said pleasantly, "and what have you been doing all the morning?"

"Winifred has been finishing her story," said Lulu, "and I've been making a bureau cover for the fair. We came down to read our stories to Aunt Daisy, but if you're reading to her now we can go away, and do it another time."

"No, indeed," said Lord Carresford, "I am sure Miss Warren would much prefer your reading to mine, but may I not be permitted to hear the stories too?"

Lulu hesitated, and glanced at Winifred.

"We don't usually like to have grown-up people read our things," she said doubtfully, "but you've been so very kind to us—shall we do it, Winifred?"

"I'd rather go home, and let you read them both," said Winifred, with a rather wistful glance in the direction of the distant hotel. "I guess I'd better go home, any way. Mother's very busy sewing for the fair, and she might want me to help her, you know."

"No, she won't," said Lulu confidently; "mamma is with her, and grown-up ladies always like to be by themselves when they sew, don't they, Aunt Daisy?"

"I don't know, I am sure," said Miss Warren, laughing, "but I really think Winifred had better stay here. You ought not to mind letting Lord Carresford hear your story, Winnie; think of all the stories he has told you himself."

"Yes, and remember how kind he was that day on the yacht," put in Lulu. "If he hadn't come to help us we might have all been drowned. I think we each ought to do something to give him pleasure."

"But it wouldn't give him pleasure to hear my silly old story," Winifred protested, blushing.

Lord Carresford insisted, however, that nothing could possibly give him greater pleasure at that moment, and Winifred, being a very good-natured, obliging little girl, made no further objections, only begging that Lulu's story might be read first. So the two little girls settled themselves comfortably on the piazza steps, and their elders prepared to listen.

"My story is called 'The Discovery of New Haven,'" remarked Lulu, with an air of pride, as she unfolded her manuscript. "Shall I begin now, Aunt Daisy?"

Miss Warren nodded; Lord Carresford lighted a cigar, and Lulu began.

"THE DISCOVERY OF NEW HAVEN

"Once there were two little girls, whose names were Lillie and Violet. Their home was in a beautiful country place called Haven. Lillie and Violet each had a pony of her own, besides a great many other wonderful things, including gardens, rabbits, and beautiful toys. Their father and mother were very good, religious people, and though they were rich themselves, they were not forgetful of the poor. They wished their little girls to grow up to be noble women.

"One evening after Lillie and Violet had gone to bed, and their father and mother—whose names were Mr. and Mrs. Lafayette—were sitting together in their beautiful parlor all furnished in velvet and gold, Mr. Lafayette suddenly paused in the middle of a piece he was playing on the pianola, and said:

"'My dear, I have thought of a most beautiful plan. Let us go to the city to-morrow, and look for two little poor children, and bring them home with us to be companions to our little girls. It is time they began to learn to make other people happy.'

"Mrs. Lafayette was delighted with this suggestion, and the next morning they started for the city.

"The scene now changes to a dirty, crowded city street——

"Don't you think that's a nice expression, Aunt Daisy, 'the scene now changes'? I got it out of 'Tales from Scott.'"

"It sounds a little like Scott, I think," Miss Warren said, smiling, and Lulu went on.

"The scene now changes to a dirty, crowded city street, where Joe and Nannie, two poor little beggar children, were busily engaged in selling matches and shoe lacings. Joe and Nannie were very poor indeed. Their father and mother were dead, and ever since they were two and three years old they had been obliged to take care of themselves. They did not even sleep in a house, but generally passed their nights in areas with their heads pillowed on the cold stone steps. It was often very uncomfortable, especially in winter, but they were very brave, cheerful children, and no one had ever heard one word of complaint from their lips. They were also very clean, and would often go to the free baths without being told.

"One very hot day in summer, when Joe and Nannie were standing on a corner, wishing most earnestly that some one would stop and buy their matches and shoe lacings a car suddenly stopped just in front of them and an elegantly dressed lady and gentleman got out."

"Don't you think it was rather poor taste in the lady and gentleman to be so elegantly dressed under the circumstances?" Aunt Daisy asked, with difficulty restraining a desire to laugh.

Lulu looked a little discomfited.

"It sounds pretty," she said. "I really don't think it matters, Aunt Daisy, as it's only a story."

"The children went up to them and asked them to please buy some of their things, but the lady, with a most beautiful smile, said:

"'Come with us, dear children, and we will take you to a much nicer place than you have ever seen in your poor, forsaken little lives.'

"Joe and Nannie, wondering very much, followed the elegant lady and gentleman, for they trusted them at once. When they came to the station, Mr. Lafayette bought tickets, and then they all got into the train that was to take them to Haven. The children had never been in a train before, and at first they were very much frightened, but their kind new friends smiled reassuringly upon them, and their fears were soon calmed.

"Lillie and Violet were very much surprised when they saw their father and mother returning from the city with two strange, ragged children, but matters were quickly explained to them, and then Mrs. Lafayette said:

"'We will first take your new companions upstairs, and dress them in some of your clothes, and then you may take them for a walk, and show them some of the beauties of the country they have come to live in.'

"So when Joe and Nannie had been neatly dressed, the children all went out together, each rich child holding the hand of a poor one. Everything was a joy and a wonder to Joe and Nannie, and they had never been so happy in their lives. They walked a long distance, much further than even Lillie or Violet had ever been before, and at last they came to a great forest. It was very beautiful, and so wild that the children loved it, and they all sat down to rest.

"Suddenly they heard a strange sound; it was the distant roar of a lion. Lillie and Violet were frightened, and wanted to run home, but Joe and Nannie looked at each other with shining eyes, and Joe cried joyfully:

"'That is the roar of a lion, so this must be an uncivilized country. Perhaps it has never before been discovered, and if so we have discovered it, and it will belong to us.'

"Then Joe and Nannie embraced each other, and they all hurried home.

"When Mr. Lafayette heard of the adventure, he told them that they had indeed made a great discovery, for no one had ever before taken possession of that wild tract of country.

"After that they all went to Washington, and the President gave Joe a claim to the undiscovered country.

"I don't know just what a claim is, but I read about it in a book.

"Then they came back again, and Joe and Nannie took possession of their vast domain, and because they wanted to show the Lafayettes how grateful they were for all their kindness, they christened their new kingdom, 'New

Haven.' In time they became very rich and powerful, and Joe married an Indian princess, and Nannie married a great duke."

"You ought to have had Joe marry one of the Lafayette girls," Lord Carresford said, laughing, as Lulu paused, and began folding up her manuscript. "It would have been another little proof of his gratitude, you know."

"I thought of that," said Lulu, "but an Indian princess sounded so pretty. Now, Winifred, it's your turn."

"My story isn't nearly as nice as yours," said Winifred modestly; "are you sure you really want me to read it?"

"Quite sure," said Lord Carresford and Miss Warren both together.

Winifred's cheeks were hot, and her heart was beating uncomfortably, but she made a mighty effort to steady her voice, and unfolding her paper, began to read very fast indeed.

"THE INDIAN

"Once upon a time there was a little girl named Rosalie. She had an older brother named John, and she had a father but not a mother.

"One day she was in the garden playing with her brother, when she suddenly saw a very curious-looking figure coming towards them through the trees. She paused for a moment in amazement, and then called, 'Brother.'

"'What is it, Rosalie?' said her brother.

"'What is that, Brother? Look at that awful thing coming towards us across the field.'

"'That is an Indian, Rosalie. Let us run to the house, and tell father.'

"They ran to the house as fast as they could, and told their father. When their father came out he said in a stern tone. 'Where is that strange figure that you saw, Rosalie?'

"Rosalie looked all around, and then said: 'There, father; he is up in that tree. I see his red blanket.'

"'That is an Indian, Rosalie, coming here to camp. I will get rid of him. Go into the house, and do your lessons.'

"So Rosalie went into the house and did her lessons. When her father came in she asked, 'How did you get rid of him, father?'

"Then her father answered: 'I did not get rid of him, Rosalie. He was John, the coachman, coming home from the village with some red blankets. Neither was it an Indian you saw in the tree, but only a red heron, and remember, I do not want you ever again to tell me a thing until you are quite sure it is true. Now, run off and play.'—THE END."

"A very nice little story," said Miss Warren, smiling approvingly, as Winifred paused; "I shall certainly use it in my book."

"I wanted her to make it longer," observed Lulu regretfully, "but she said she couldn't possibly think of another word to say."

[NOTE.—The above stories were written word for word by two little girls eight and ten years of age.]

"It has a good moral at any rate," laughed Lord Carresford, "and that is more than can be said for every story. Are you going in, Miss Warren?"

"I have a little writing to do this morning," the blind lady explained, rising, and folding up her knitting as she spoke, "and Mrs. Randall is coming in half an hour for my music lesson. Are you going to the beach, Lulu?"

"No; mamma thinks it too hot on the beach to-day, and Mrs. Hamilton doesn't want Winifred to go either. We've asked Betty and Jack over here, and mamma says we may have lemonade and cookies by and by."

"Lulu," said Lord Carresford, as the screen door closed behind Miss Warren, "who is Mrs. Randall?"

"Why, don't you know? She's Betty and Jack's mother, and she gives Aunt Daisy music lessons. She's a splendid music teacher, every one says so."

"I did not know their name was Randall," said Lord Carresford, looking interested, though a little troubled as well. "They are English, are they not?"

"Mrs. Randall is, but Betty and Jack were born in this country. Their father died when Jack was only two, and they were very poor. Mrs. Randall doesn't like to have them talk about it; she's a very proud lady."

At that moment Winifred announced that the Randalls were approaching, and the two little girls ran off across the lawn to meet their friends.

"Jack," said Lord Carresford, sitting down beside the little boy, when he had assisted in placing him comfortably in the big steamer chair, "did you say anything to your mother about what I told you yesterday afternoon?"

Jack's eyes fell, and the color rose in his cheeks.

"N—no, sir," he faltered; "I told Betty, and we decided it would be better not to say anything to mother about it. You see, she'd be so very sorry not to be able to let me have the lessons."

"And have you no relations who could afford to help you—no uncles or aunts, for instance?"

Jack shook his head.

"We haven't any relations at all," he said mournfully, "only an uncle in England, and we don't know him."

"Don't know him, eh; but your mother knows him, doesn't she?"

"Oh, yes, at least she used to; he's her brother, you know, but we've never seen him, and mother doesn't like to have us talk much about him, because it makes her sad."

"What is your uncle's name?" Lord Carresford spoke quickly, and there was a kind of suppressed excitement in his manner, which surprised Jack very much.

"His name is Mr. John Stanhope," said Jack proudly; "I am named for him. My grandfather was General Stanhope, and we have another uncle, who is a—but, oh, I forgot; mother said we mustn't talk about him."

Lord Carresford rose hurriedly. He had suddenly grown very pale.

"Is your mother at home now?" he asked in a voice so odd and unsteady that Jack stared at him in growing bewilderment.

"Yes, I think she is," he said slowly; "she's coming over here pretty soon to give Miss Warren her music lesson. Don't you feel very well, sir?"

"Yes, yes, my boy, I am all right. I must see your mother, that is all. I—I think I used to know her long ago in England."

"Did you really?" inquired Jack, his face brightening. "Oh, I'm very glad. Perhaps you knew our Uncle Jack too, and can tell us where he lives."

At that moment Betty's voice was heard from the other end of the piazza. "Here comes mother, Jack."

Lord Carresford turned his head; took a few hurried steps forward, and then stood still, gazing at the figure of the tall lady rapidly approaching across the lawn. He was very white, but there was a strange, glad light in his eyes. All unconscious of the stranger's eager scrutiny the lady had almost reached the piazza steps before the sound of Betty's voice caused her to raise her eyes. Then suddenly her glance met that of Lord Carresford, and, with a low cry, she started forward with both hands outstretched.

"Jack," she gasped, "oh, Jack!" And then all at once her strength seemed to fail her, and she sank down on the lowest step, shaking from head to foot, while every particle of color went out of her face.

Ten minutes later Mrs. Bell and Mrs. Hamilton, who were spending a pleasant morning together in the latter's room at the hotel, were startled by the sudden and violent opening of the door, and the precipitate entrance of Lulu and Winifred, both hatless, breathless, and almost beside themselves with excitement.

"Oh, mamma, mamma," cried Lulu, flinging herself upon her astonished mother, "the most wonderful, exciting, extraordinary thing has happened! Lord Carresford is kissing Mrs. Randall on our piazza, and she's got her arms round his neck, and is laughing and crying both at the same time. We don't know what it all means, but we told Aunt Daisy, and she said we'd better come for you."

CHAPTER XVI

UNCLE JACK

"I think it's the most interesting thing that ever happened in all our lives," remarked Lulu in a tone of conviction. "To think of Lord Carresford's turning out to be Betty's own uncle, and we never knowing a thing about it."

It was late in the afternoon, and the two little girls were sitting in their favorite spot on the bathing house steps, discussing the events of the day.

"It is very interesting," said Winifred, with a little sigh of content. "It's really quite like a book thing; don't you think so?"

"Just as interesting things happen really as they do in books," said Lulu with superior wisdom. "Aunt Daisy says truth is stranger than fiction, and she ought to know, because she writes books herself. Lots of interesting things have happened to us, but I don't think anything was ever quite so wonderful as this one."

"I should think Betty and Jack would be just crazy. I know I should be if a lord turned out to be my uncle, especially if he were as nice as Lord Carresford."

"Just think," said Winifred reflectively, "the Rossiters said their mother was surprised we were allowed to be so intimate with Betty, because we didn't know anything about her family. Won't they be surprised when they hear all about it. I don't suppose the Randalls will be any different now they know they've got a lord for a relation, though it would be enough to make some people rather stuck up; don't you think it would? You remember how stuck up Elsie Carleton was that time her uncle's sister-in-law married a duke's son."

"Bother Elsie Carleton," retorted Lulu with scorn. "Betty isn't that kind of a person, or Jack either."

"Do you suppose they'll go to England and live in a castle?" Winifred inquired in a rather awestruck tone.

"I suppose so; Lord Carresford is dreadfully rich, you know, and if he shouldn't ever happen to get married, why, Jack would inherit his title, and be a lord too."

"He'd rather be an artist, I think," said Winifred,i "or a general, like his grandfather. Oh, here they come; now they'll tell us all about it."

There was certainly no appearance of lofty superiority about the Randalls, as they came hurrying along the sand, Betty pushing Jack's go-cart as usual, and their greeting to their friends was very much as it had been that morning, before they had, as Lulu expressed it, "found out they had a lord for a relation."

"We're so awfully glad you've come," said Lulu joyfully, helping Jack out of the go-cart, while Winifred hastily improvised a seat for him in the sand. "We wanted to go over to see you, but mamma and Mrs. Hamilton said we mustn't. They thought your mother and Lord Carresford might have a great many things to talk about, and wouldn't want us around."

"They've been talking all the afternoon in mother's room," said Betty, "and Jack and I stayed out on the piazza, but a little while ago they called us in, and told us about everything. You can't think how pretty mother looks; her eyes are just shining, and she's got such a lovely color in her cheeks."

"I should think she would be glad," said Lulu comprehendingly. "Does it feel funny to be so very rich, Betty?"

Betty laughed and blushed.

"We're not so very rich," she said modestly. "We shouldn't have been rich at all, only that our grandfather was sorry just before he died, and wanted to make another will, and leave some of his money to mother. He told Uncle Jack, and he was very glad, and sent right off for a lawyer, but our grandfather, who was very ill, didn't live till the lawyer came. But Uncle Jack promised he would try to find mother, and make it all right about the money. That's what he came to this country for, but, you see, the trouble was he didn't know what part of America father and mother had come to. He didn't even know that father was dead. Mother never heard Lord Carresford's name until she saw him, standing on your piazza, but even if she had she wouldn't have known he was Uncle Jack, because she had never heard of the other two Lord Carresfords being dead."

"I think it's the loveliest thing I ever heard of," said Winifred, "just think, Jack, you'll live in a castle with a park, like little Lord Fauntleroy."

"And mother won't have to work any more," said Jack, with sparkling eyes, "and Betty will be a lady when she grows up, the kind of lady I wanted her to be. Oh, I'm so happy, I feel as if I should like to fly."

"When father and mother first came home from California I used to think it must be a dream," said Winifred, "but it was all true, and so is this lovely thing about your Uncle Jack." And Winifred slipped her kind little hand lovingly into that of her friend.

Jack gave the small fingers an appreciative squeeze.

"There's only one thing I'm sorry about," he whispered shyly, "and that is that when we go to England to live we won't see you any more, not unless you come over there to see us some time."

"Perhaps we shall," said Winifred hopefully. "If we do will you ask us to stay at your castle?"

"Of course, and—I say, Winnie, when I grow up—I shall be able to walk like other people then, you know—I'll come over here to see you, and— and I'll marry you if you want me to. I like you better than any other girl in the world except Betty."

"There's mother beckoning to me; I must go right away," exclaimed Winifred, starting to her feet, and looking extremely red. "Good-night, Jack; good-night, Betty and Lulu." And away flew the little girl, never pausing or looking back until she was safely at her mother's side.

"I wonder what made Winifred leave in such a hurry," remarked Lulu, looking after her friend in some surprise, but Jack did not offer any explanation.

"Well, Jack, my boy," said Lord Carresford, joining his little nephew on the boarding house piazza that evening after dinner, and laying his hand affectionately on his shoulder, "what makes you look so serious? No more difficulties about drawing lessons, eh?"

"Oh, Uncle Jack, I'm so very happy; I was just thinking how beautiful everything is, and I was wishing——"

"Well, what were you wishing?" his uncle asked smiling, as Jack paused.

"Only that everybody else in the world might be happy too."

"Rather a big wish, isn't it, my boy? but your mother and I have been talking things over just now, and we have a plan, which I think may give some of your little friends pleasure. You know you are to leave this house the day after to-morrow; now where should you like best to go?"

"On board the yacht," said Jack unhesitatingly.

"Well, that is just where we are thinking of going. I want to take your mother for a short cruise to the coast of Maine, and I propose that we invite the Bells and Hamiltons to go with us. I believe Dr. Bell and Mr. Hamilton both talk of taking vacations next week."

Jack's eyes danced with delight.

"I think," he said, with a sigh of deep content, "that it would be the very nicest thing that could possibly happen."

That evening Lord Carresford had a long talk with his friends Dr. and Mrs. Bell, the result of which was that three days later "his lordship's" yacht was gliding smoothly out of the harbor, bound for the coast of Maine, and carrying on board four very happy children.

"When I said I wished I could go to sea in a yacht the day we were shipwrecked, I never dreamed it would really happen," remarked Lulu, surveying her new surroundings with an expression of intense satisfaction. "I think it's really quite remarkable the way things happen sometimes."

"I wish your mother and aunt could have come too," said Winifred a little regretfully. "I don't believe anybody could really be seasick in this lovely place."

"It isn't always as smooth as this," returned Lulu, remembering past experiences of Father Ocean. "You see it isn't very comfortable for people to go on yachts when they are apt to be seasick. Mamma and Aunt Daisy were both dreadfully seasick when we went to Europe."

"I hope you won't be homesick," said Betty anxiously. "You haven't ever been away from your mother before, have you?"

"No, but I sha'n't be, I know. It's only for a week, and I'm going to write her a letter every day, and one to Aunt Daisy too. Then I've got papa, you know, and Mrs. Hamilton is going to take care of me."

"And no one could possibly be homesick with my mother," added Winifred, with an adoring glance at Mrs. Hamilton, who was sitting near by, chatting with Mrs. Randall.

"Well, young people, are you having a good time?" Lord Carresford inquired, sauntering up to the group.

"Yes, indeed we are," came in chorus from all four voices.

"Come with me to the other side of the boat, and we'll have a last look at Sandy Hook. Do you want to come too, Jack?"

"No, thank you," said the little boy, smiling happily; "I'd rather sit here; it's so comfortable."

"I'm the happiest boy in the world," said Jack

Lord Carresford and the three little girls moved away to the other side of the yacht, and were soon joined by Dr. Bell and Mr. and Mrs. Hamilton.

"Are you happy, Jack, darling?" Mrs. Randall whispered, bending down to kiss the radiant little face, when the two were left alone together.

"Oh, mother, I'm the happiest boy in the world," said Jack, softly stroking his mother's hand, and laying his cheek against it. "All the beautiful things I've ever dreamed about have come true. I used to think that if I could only walk I would never wish for anything else, and now that's happened, and such lots and lots of other nice things too. We've found Uncle Jack, and I'm going to be an Englishman and an artist; and Betty's going to be a lady. Oh, mother, dear, doesn't it all seem just like a fairy story that's come true?"

THE END